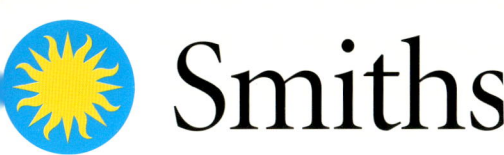 

Smiths
ENGAGEMENT CALENDAR

© 2024 Smithsonian Institution

All rights reserved. No part of this publication may be reproduced or transmitted in any form or by any means, electronic or mechanical, including photocopying, recording, or information storage or retrieval system, without permission in writing from the publishers.

February 16: © Brian Lanker Archive
March 2: © Derek Fordjour, courtesy of David Kordansky Gallery. Photo by Ron Amstutz for the Hirshhorn Museum and Sculpture Garden
July 27: © Audrey Flack
September 14: © Lesley Vance, courtesy of David Kordansky Gallery
November 16: © Manuel Vega

This calendar may be purchased for educational, business, or sales promotional use. For information, please write: Special Markets Department, Smithsonian Books, PO Box 37012, MRC 513, Washington, DC 20013.

Published by Smithsonian Books
www.smithsonianbooks.com

Senior Editor: Jaime Schwender
Editor: Julie Huggins
Copyedited by Tom Fredrickson
Designed by Robert L. Wiser

Printed in China, not at government expense.

A special thanks to Jorge Alemán, Kimberly Arcand, Lisa Austin, Heidi Austreng, Erin Beasley, Marisa Bourgoin, Logan Clark, Rhys Conlon, Ren Cooper, Linda Currie, Miriam Doutriaux, Laura Duff, Linette Dutari, Marshall Emery, Angela Ferragamo, Cory Grace, Migs Grove, Laura Harger, Paula Healy, Sarah Hedean, Pamela Henson, Elisa Hough, Janice Hussain, Amy Hutchins, Betsy Johnson, Beth King, Lauren Kolodkin, Fernanda Luppani, Deane Madsen, Julia Murphy, Timothy Nolan, Cecilia Peterson, Kay Peterson, Jim Preston, Kristen Quarles, Douglas Remley, Erin Rushing, Jennifer Schneider, Jennifer Schommer, Marie Sicola, Brad Simpson, Tellie Simpson, Marc Sklar, Riche Sorensen, Tanya Thrasher, Kayleigh Walters, Megan Watzke, Kelly Williamson, and Jennifer Zoon.

Photographs are of objects in the collections of the museums and research facilities that make up the Smithsonian. Special thanks to Smithsonian photographers Jorge Alemán, Ernest Amoroso, Mark Avino, Rick Coulby, James Di Loreto, Harold Dorwin, Matt Flynn, Katherine Fogden (Mohawk), Brittany M. Hance, Donald E. Hurlbert, Alex Jamison, Franko Khoury, Hannele Lahti, Eric Long, Lucia RM Martino, Jaclyn Nash, Roshan Patel, Jim Preston, Jessica Scott, and Rich Strauss.

Equinox, solstice, and moon phase dates are given according to Eastern Standard Time or Eastern Daylight Saving Time as applicable.

● New Moon   ◐ First Quarter   ○ Full Moon   ◑ Last Quarter

For previsit planning material, please contact: Smithsonian Information, Smithsonian Institution, SI Building, Room 153, PO Box 37012, MRC 010, Washington, DC 20013-7012, 202-633-1000 (voice). Send email inquiries to info@si.edu. Visit us on the web at www.si.edu/visit.

To order Smithsonian engagement calendars: Please visit www.smithsonianstore.com or call 1-800-322-0344. Shipping and handling charges will apply.

Front Cover:
Utagawa Hiroshige
(1797–1858)
View of Shiba Coast (Shibaura No Fukei), 1856
From the series *One Hundred Famous Views of Edo*
Edo period, Japan
Woodblock print
in colored ink on paper
14 × 9½ in. (35.6 × 24.1 cm)
Gift of the Estate of Mrs. Robert H. Patterson
Cooper Hewitt,
Smithsonian Design Museum

One Hundred Famous Views of Edo is a series of 119 ukiyo-e prints, a genre that flourished in Japan from the 17th through the 19th centuries. This image of the Shiba coast along Edo Bay contains many examples of the use of perspective, a hallmark of the series.

Star-Forming Region 30 Doradus in X-ray and Infrared Light
Digital photograph made from X-ray light detected by NASA's Chandra X-ray Observatory and infrared light detected by NASA's James Webb Space Telescope, January 9, 2023
Chandra X-ray Observatory / James Webb Space Telescope
Smithsonian Astrophysical Observatory

The largest and brightest region of star formation in the Local Group (the galaxy group that contains the Milky Way), 30 Doradus is located in the Large Magellanic Cloud, about 170,000 light-years from Earth. It has long been studied by astronomers who want to better understand how stars like our Sun are born and evolve.

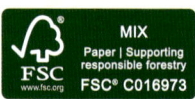

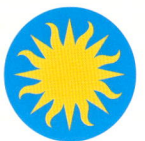

Smithsonian 2025
ENGAGEMENT CALENDAR

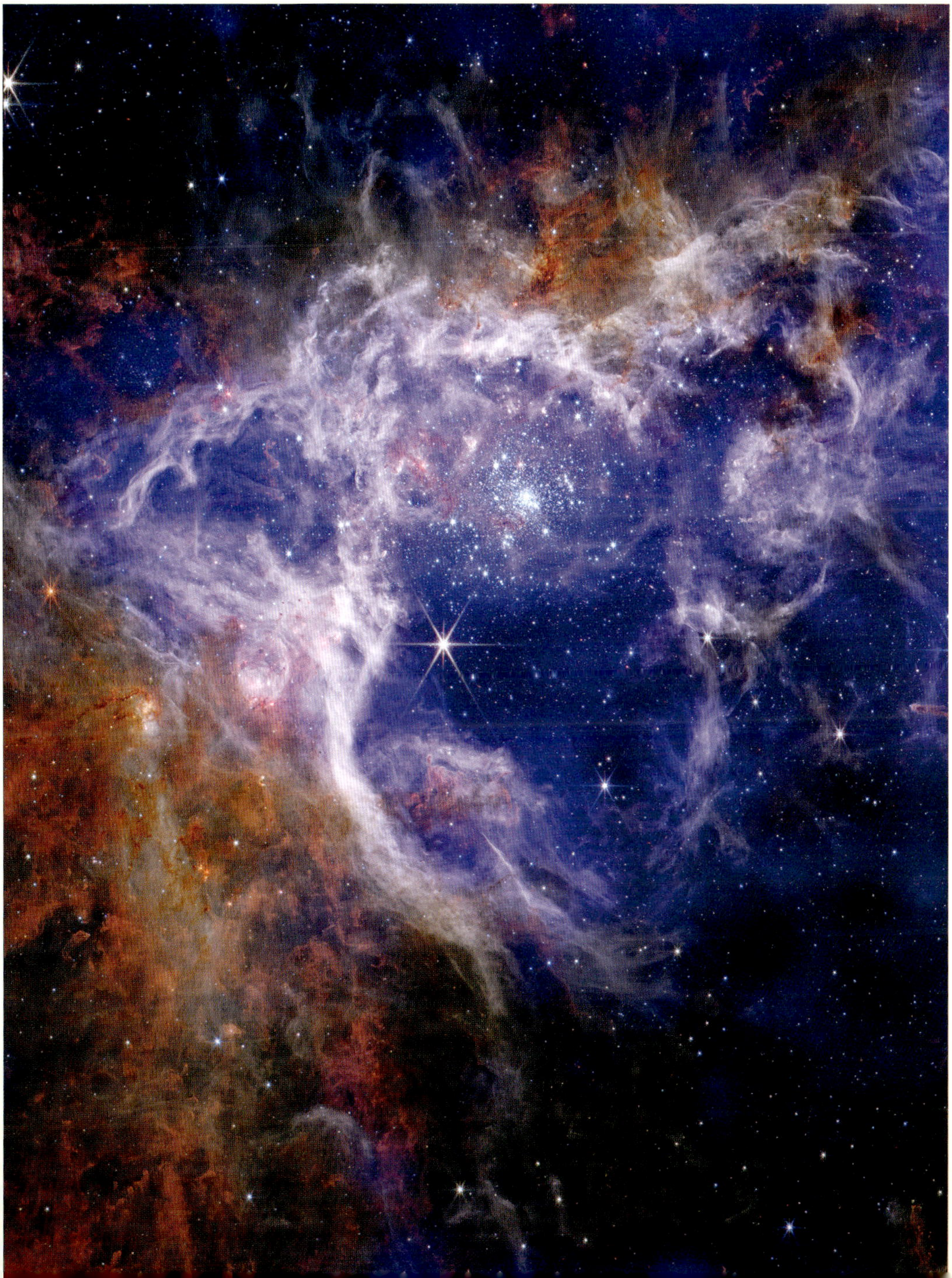

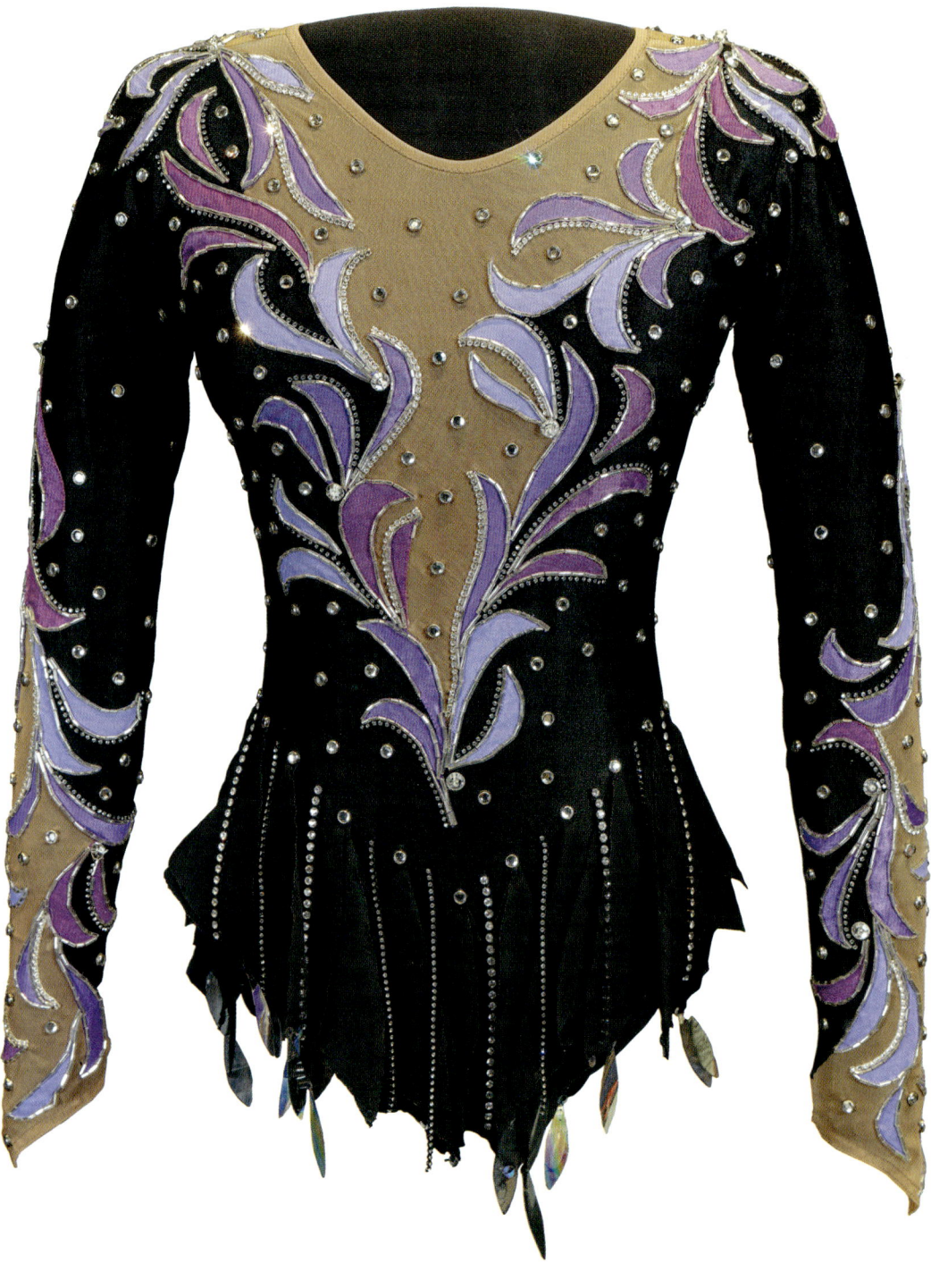

DECEMBER · JANUARY

Black-and-purple figure-skating costume worn by Debi Thomas, 1986
Designed by
Lauren MacDonald Sheehan (b. 1956)
Lycra, spandex, polyester, nylon, beads, and sequins
27 3/16 × 14 9/16 in. (69 × 37 cm)
Gift of
Debra Janine Thomas
National Museum of African American History and Culture

Debi Thomas (b. 1967) wore this costume when she won the US and World Figure Skating Championships in 1986. Thomas would go on to become the first African American to win a medal at the Winter Olympics when she won a bronze in women's singles figure skating in 1988.

DECEMBER 2024
S	M	T	W	T	F	S
1	2	3	4	5	6	7
8	9	10	11	12	13	14
15	16	17	18	19	20	21
22	23	24	25	26	27	28
29	30	31				

JANUARY
S	M	T	W	T	F	S
			1	2	3	4
5	6	7	8	9	10	11
12	13	14	15	16	17	18
19	20	21	22	23	24	25
26	27	28	29	30	31	

SUNDAY
29

MONDAY
30

NEW YEAR'S EVE

TUESDAY
31

NEW YEAR'S DAY · KWANZAA ENDS

WEDNESDAY
1

HANUKKAH ENDS (SUNDOWN)

THURSDAY
2

FRIDAY
3

SATURDAY
4

JANUARY

SUNDAY
5

MONDAY
6 ☽

TUESDAY
7

WEDNESDAY
8

THURSDAY
9

FRIDAY
10

SATURDAY
11

Hisako Hibi (1907–1991)
Floating Clouds, 1944
Oil on canvas
19 1/16 × 23 in.
(48.4 × 58.4 cm)
Smithsonian American
Art Museum

Although Hisako Hibi's career spanned eight decades, her work from her internment during World War II has become her most recognizable. Despite the hardships of camp life, Hibi was especially productive during this period; from 1942 to 1945 she produced more than sixty paintings, including this one. *Floating Clouds* shows soft gray clouds hovering over austere, windowless buildings reminiscent of the "humiliating" accommodations at Tanforan Assembly Center near San Francisco, where Hibi and her husband were held with their daughter.

JANUARY
S	M	T	W	T	F	S
			1	2	3	4
5	6	7	8	9	10	11
12	13	14	15	16	17	18
19	20	21	22	23	24	25
26	27	28	29	30	31	

FEBRUARY
S	M	T	W	T	F	S
						1
2	3	4	5	6	7	8
9	10	11	12	13	14	15
16	17	18	19	20	21	22
23	24	25	26	27	28	

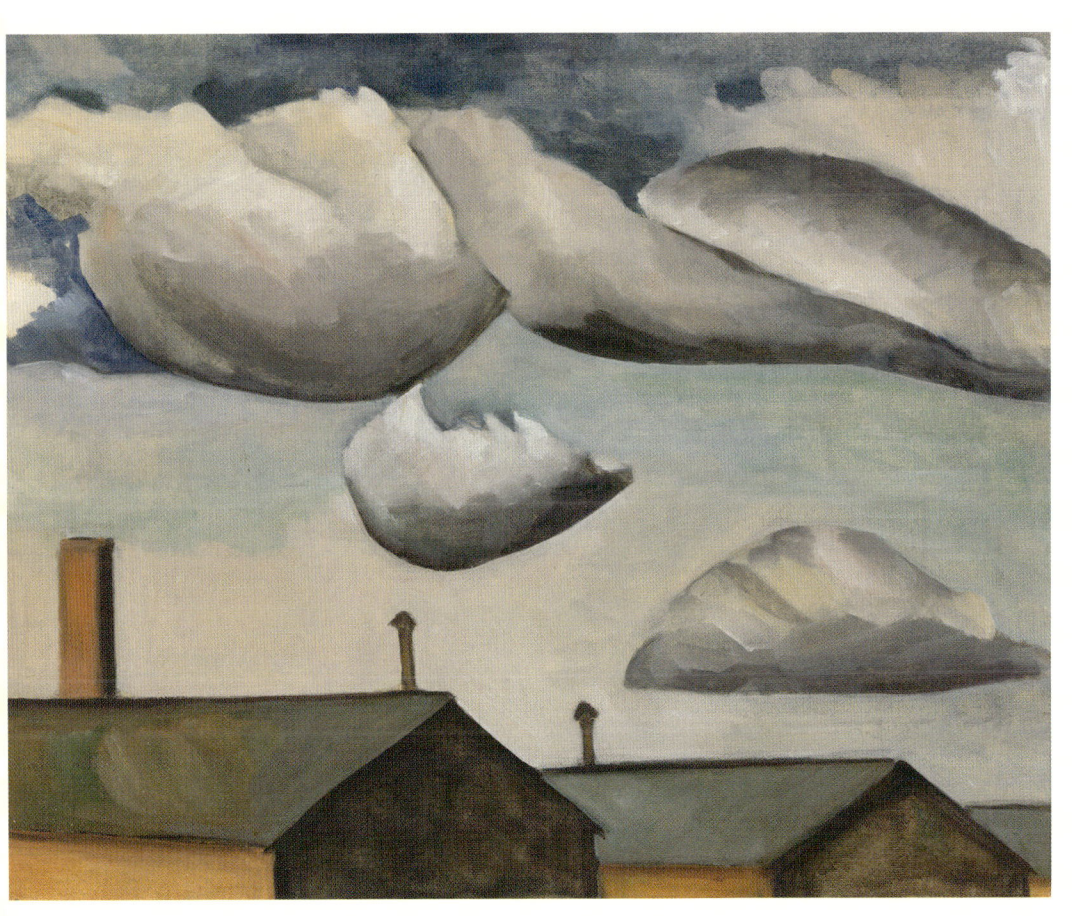

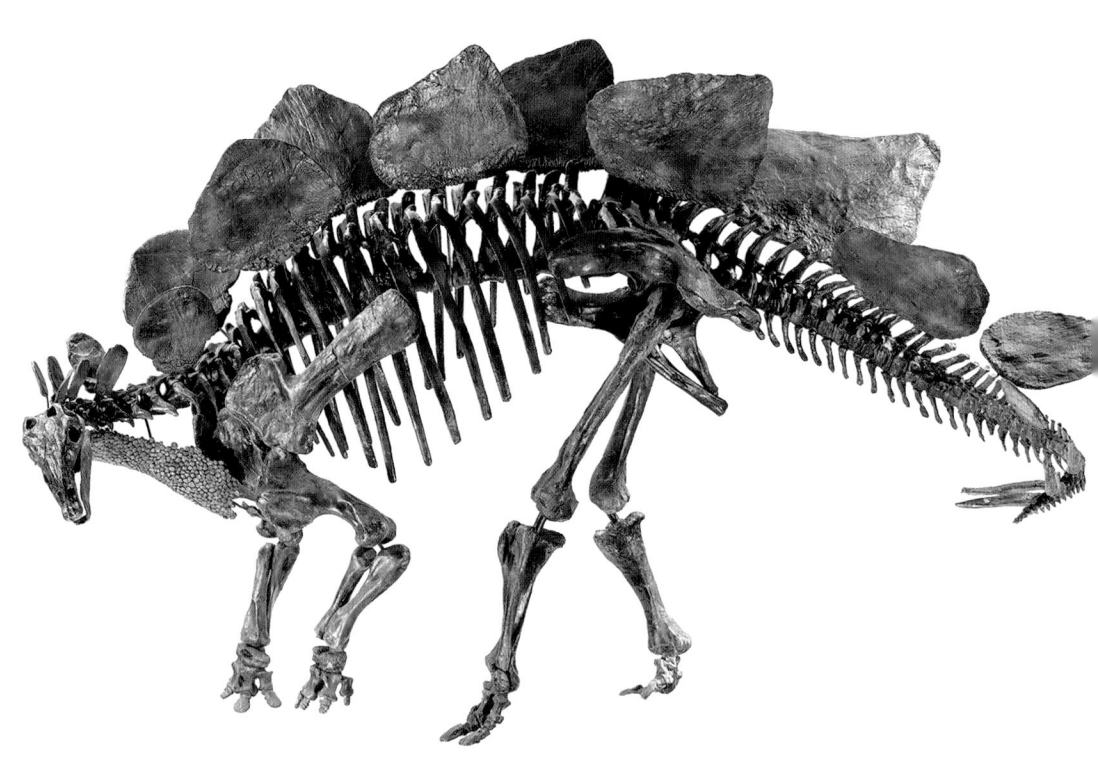

Stegosaurus stenops Marsh, 1887
Como Bluff, WY
235 × 102½ in.
(597 × 260 cm)
National Museum of Natural History

The herbivorous dinosaur *Stegosaurus* is easily recognized by its tail spikes and back plates. This skeleton, on display in the *Deep Time* exhibition, is a composite of fossil casts from the Smithsonian's vertebrate paleontology collections. Complete dinosaur skeletons are rare, so paleontologists sometimes combine bones from several individuals to create a single exhibit specimen.

JANUARY

SUNDAY	12
MONDAY	13
TUESDAY	14
WEDNESDAY	15
THURSDAY	16
FRIDAY	17
SATURDAY	18

JANUARY

S	M	T	W	T	F	S
			1	2	3	4
5	6	7	8	9	10	11
12	13	14	15	16	17	18
19	20	21	22	23	24	25
26	27	28	29	30	31	

FEBRUARY

S	M	T	W	T	F	S
						1
2	3	4	5	6	7	8
9	10	11	12	13	14	15
16	17	18	19	20	21	22
23	24	25	26	27	28	

JANUARY

SUNDAY
19

MONDAY MARTIN LUTHER KING JR. DAY
20

TUESDAY ◐
21

WEDNESDAY
22

THURSDAY
23

FRIDAY
24

SATURDAY
25

Postcard of
handloom weavers
Algeria
Published by Raphael Tuck
& Sons, c. 1905
Hand-colored collotype
3½ × 5½ in. (9 × 14 cm)
Eliot Elisofon
Photographic Archives
National Museum
of African Art

Arab women used a traditional handloom weaving method to create cloth. By passing—from one woman to another—the weft (horizontal) threads through the warp threads strung vertically on beams, they produced fabric for garments such as the coarse woolen cloak with a pointed hood called a burnouse.

JANUARY
S M T W T F S
            1 2 3 4
5 6 7 8 9 10 11
12 13 14 15 16 17 18
19 20 21 22 23 24 25
26 27 28 29 30 31

FEBRUARY
S M T W T F S
                  1
2 3 4 5 6 7 8
9 10 11 12 13 14 15
16 17 18 19 20 21 22
23 24 25 26 27 28

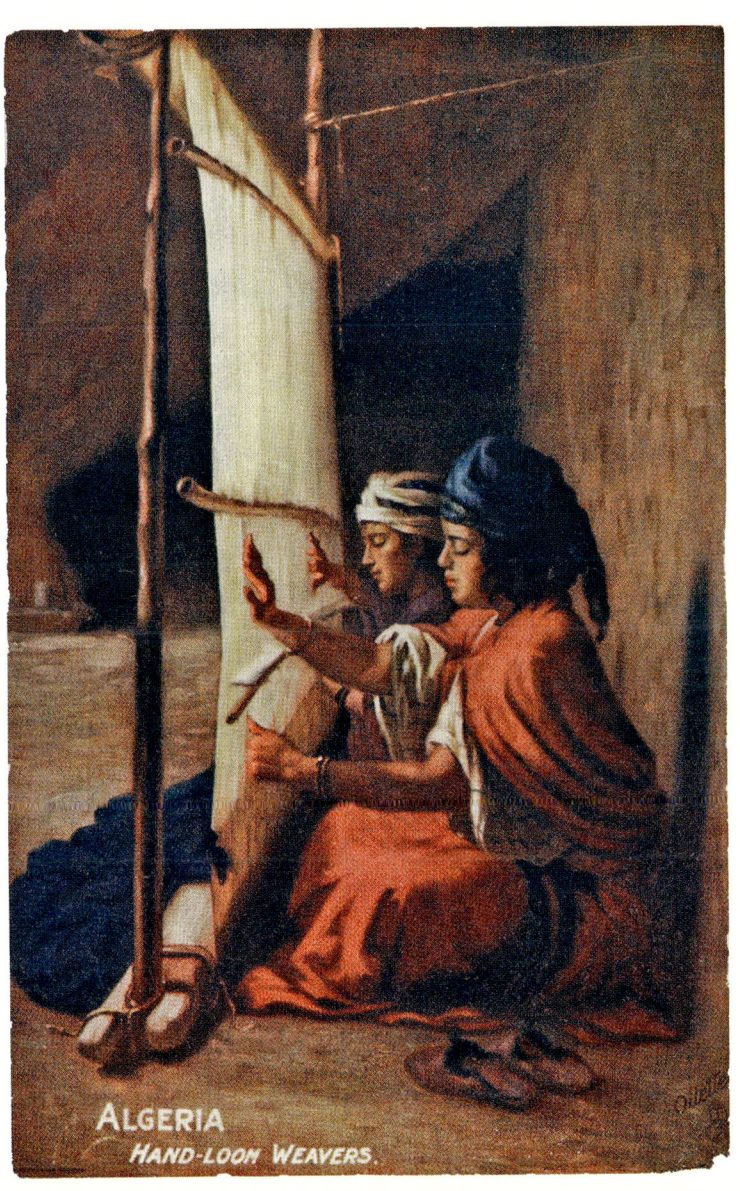

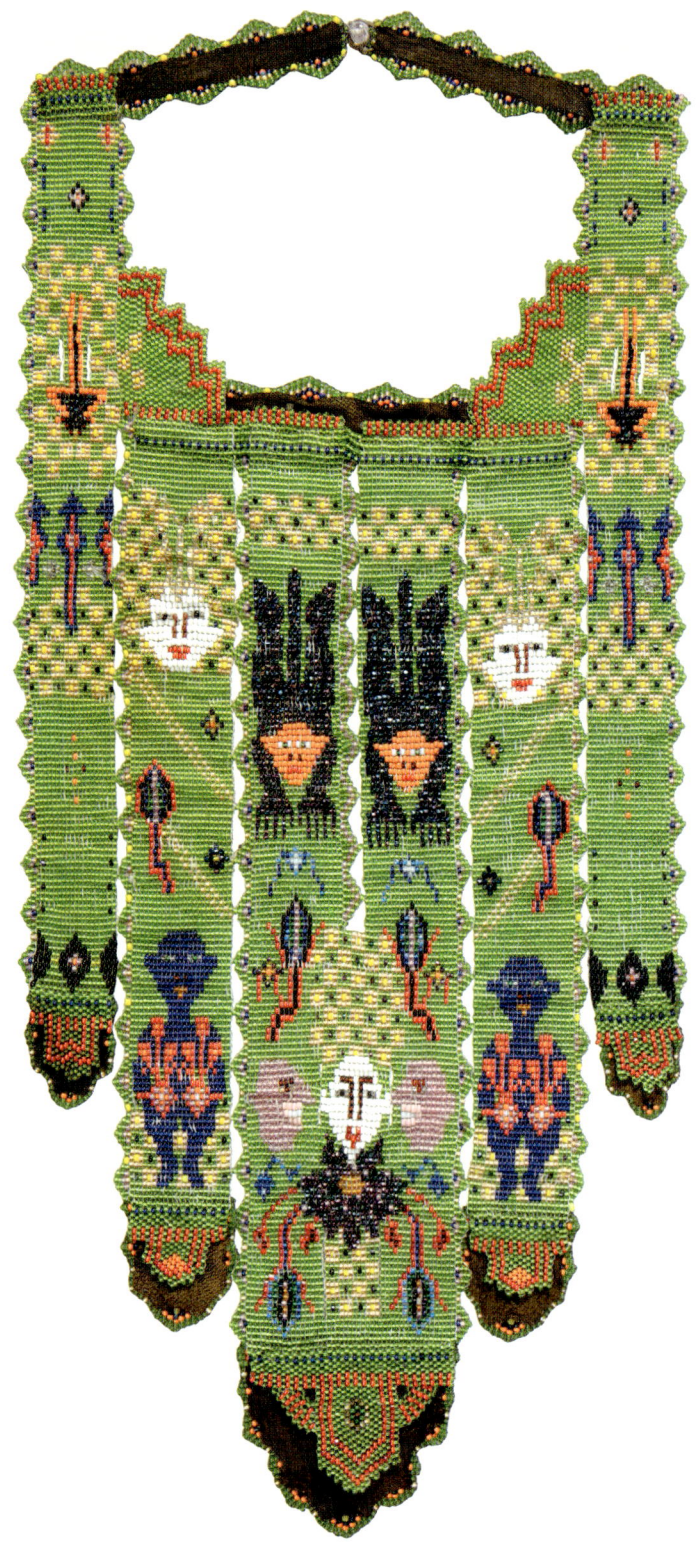

JANUARY · FEBRUARY

Joyce Scott (b. 1948)
Chinese Panthers necklace, 1979
United States
Loom- and peyote-stitched glass beads and thread
19¼ × 8⅝ × ¼ in.
(48.9 × 21.9 × 0.6 cm)
Cooper Hewitt, Smithsonian Design Museum

Joyce Scott creates beadwork objects that draw attention to pressing social and political issues. Her practice extends three generations of familial craft traditions. In this necklace, Scott colorfully wove together complex imagery including pre-Columbian motifs and mythological figures to make a powerful visual statement through jewelry.

JANUARY
S	M	T	W	T	F	S
			1	2	3	4
5	6	7	8	9	10	11
12	13	14	15	16	17	18
19	20	21	22	23	24	25
26	27	28	29	30	31	

FEBRUARY
S	M	T	W	T	F	S
						1
2	3	4	5	6	7	8
9	10	11	12	13	14	15
16	17	18	19	20	21	22
23	24	25	26	27	28	

SUNDAY
26

MONDAY
27

TUESDAY
28

● LUNAR NEW YEAR

WEDNESDAY
29

THURSDAY
30

FRIDAY
31

SATURDAY
1

FEBRUARY

SUNDAY
2

MONDAY
3

TUESDAY
4

WEDNESDAY
5   ◐

THURSDAY
6

FRIDAY
7

SATURDAY
8

Helen Hyde (1868–1919)
Going to Market, 1912
Color woodcut print
on paper
15 1/16 × 7 5/16 in.
(38.3 × 18.5 cm)
Graphic Arts Collection
National Museum
of American History

Helen Hyde traveled from San Francisco to Europe and Japan to study art. Her work in more than one medium was a response to the nineteenth-century art-and-design movement called "Japonisme." Hyde retained components of the style in her later works depicting San Francisco's Chinatown as well as Mexico, views of which she portrayed as "pervaded by a soft haze."

FEBRUARY
S	M	T	W	T	F	S
						1
2	3	4	5	6	7	8
9	10	11	12	13	14	15
16	17	18	19	20	21	22
23	24	25	26	27	28	

MARCH
S	M	T	W	T	F	S
						1
2	3	4	5	6	7	8
9	10	11	12	13	14	15
16	17	18	19	20	21	22
23	24	25	26	27	28	29
30	31					

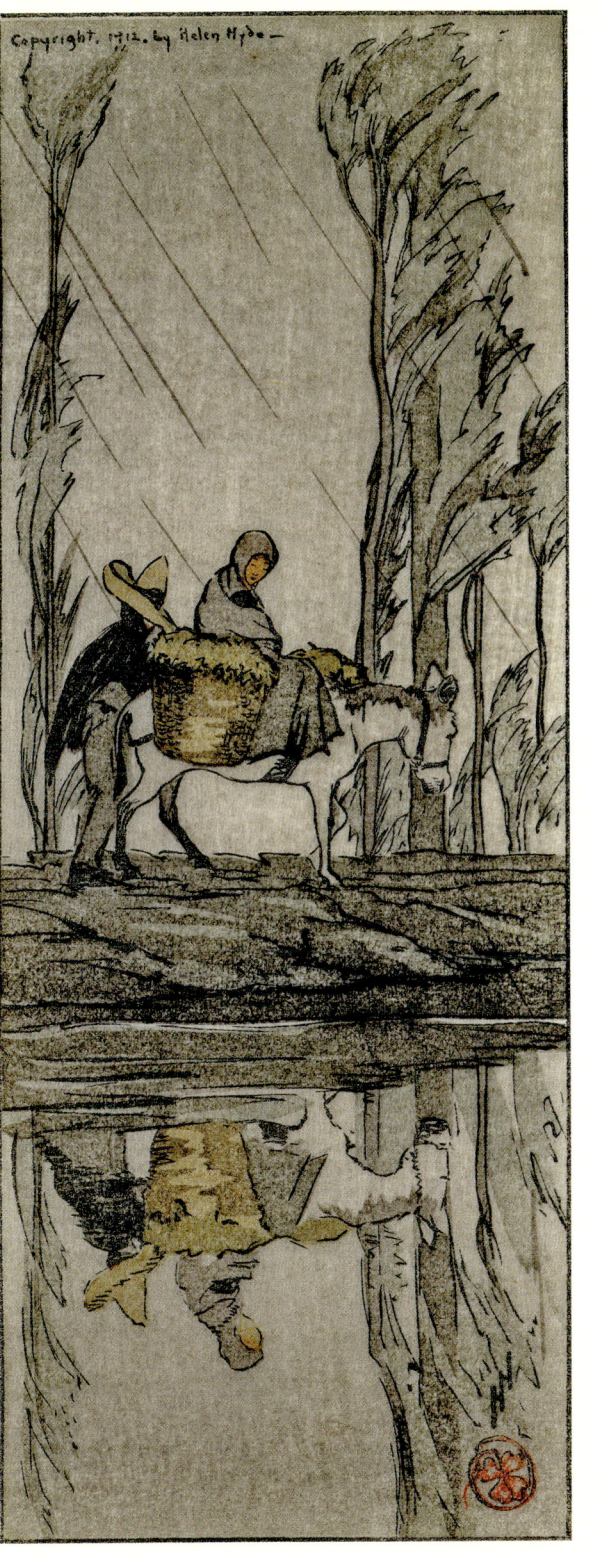

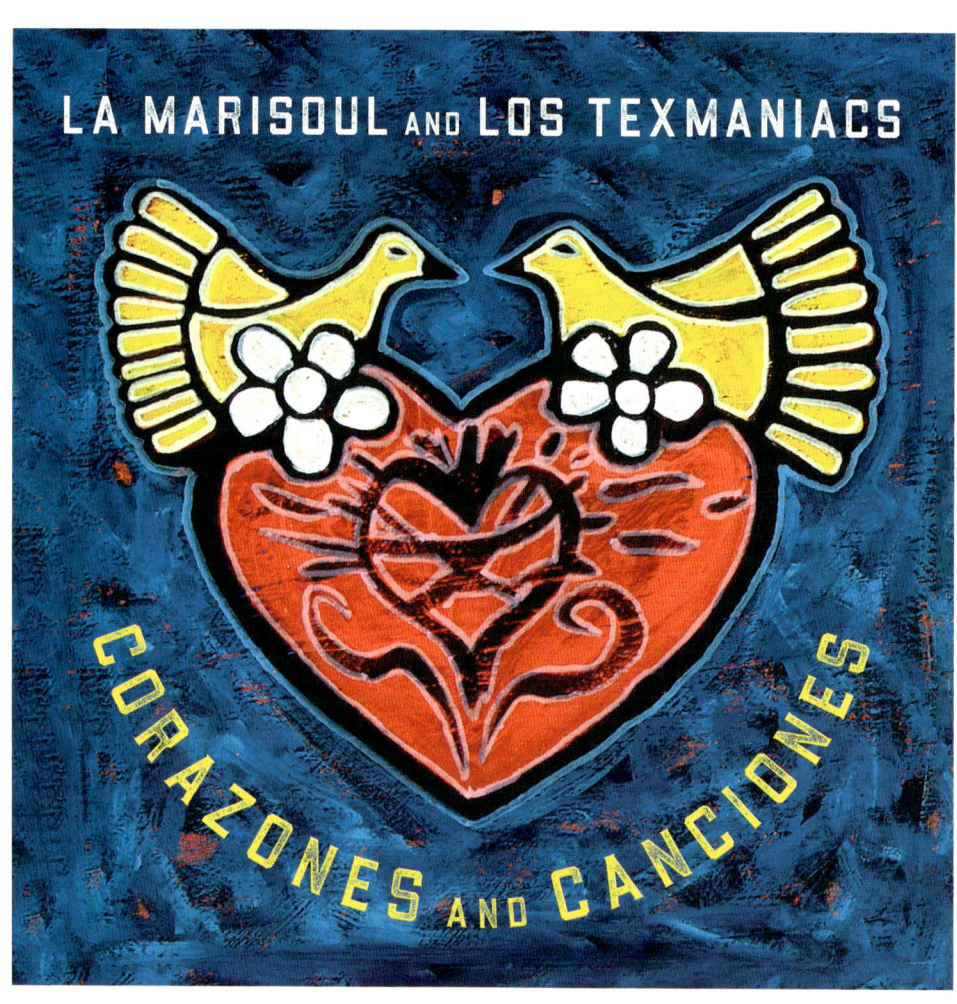

Corazones and Canciones, 2023
La Marisoul and Los Texmaniacs
Cover artwork by José Ramírez
Cover design by Cooley Design Lab
5½ × 4¾ in. (14 × 12 cm)
Smithsonian Folkways Recordings
Smithsonian Center for Folklife and Cultural Heritage

In *Corazones and Canciones*, two Mexican American musical powerhouses join forces to create an album overflowing with heart and imagination. Marisol Hernández of Los Angeles—La Marisoul—and San Antonio-based Tejano conjunto group Los Texmaniacs draw from a repertoire of cherished *canciones rancheras* and *boleros*. Special guest Little Joe Hernández adds his trademark vocals to the melody of "Las Nubes," the song he propelled to the forefront of the Chicano movement.

FEBRUARY

S	M	T	W	T	F	S
						1
2	3	4	5	6	7	8
9	10	11	12	13	14	15
16	17	18	19	20	21	22
23	24	25	26	27	28	

MARCH

S	M	T	W	T	F	S
						1
2	3	4	5	6	7	8
9	10	11	12	13	14	15
16	17	18	19	20	21	22
23	24	25	26	27	28	29
30	31					

FEBRUARY

SUNDAY
9

MONDAY
10

TUESDAY
11

WEDNESDAY
12

THURSDAY
13

VALENTINE'S DAY   **FRIDAY**
14

SATURDAY
15

FEBRUARY

SUNDAY
16

MONDAY — PRESIDENTS' DAY
17

TUESDAY
18

WEDNESDAY
19

THURSDAY ◐
20

FRIDAY
21

SATURDAY
22

Brian Lanker (1947–2011)
Cicely Tyson, 1988
Gelatin silver print
28⅛ × 28 in.
(71.4 × 71.1 cm)
Partial gift of Lynda Lanker
National Portrait Gallery

An actor of great depth and sensitivity, Cicely Tyson (1924–2021) rejected roles that perpetuated negative racial stereotypes, choosing instead to portray admirable Black women. Her most memorable roles included the indomitable wife of a sharecropper in the film *Sounder* (1972) and the title character in the television drama *The Autobiography of Miss Jane Pittman* (1974).

FEBRUARY

S	M	T	W	T	F	S
						1
2	3	4	5	6	7	8
9	10	11	12	13	14	15
16	17	18	19	20	21	22
23	24	25	26	27	28	

MARCH

S	M	T	W	T	F	S
						1
2	3	4	5	6	7	8
9	10	11	12	13	14	15
16	17	18	19	20	21	22
23	24	25	26	27	28	29
30	31					

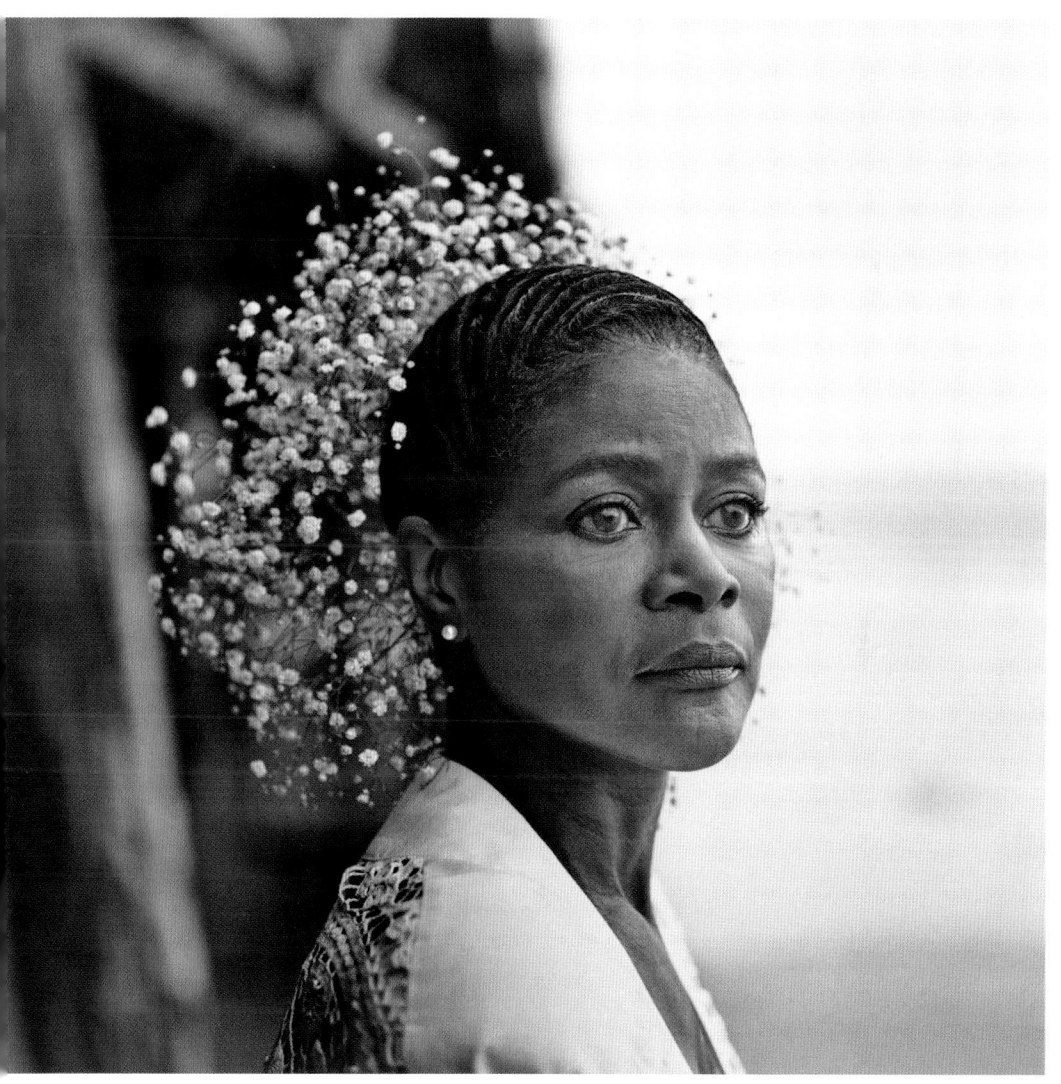

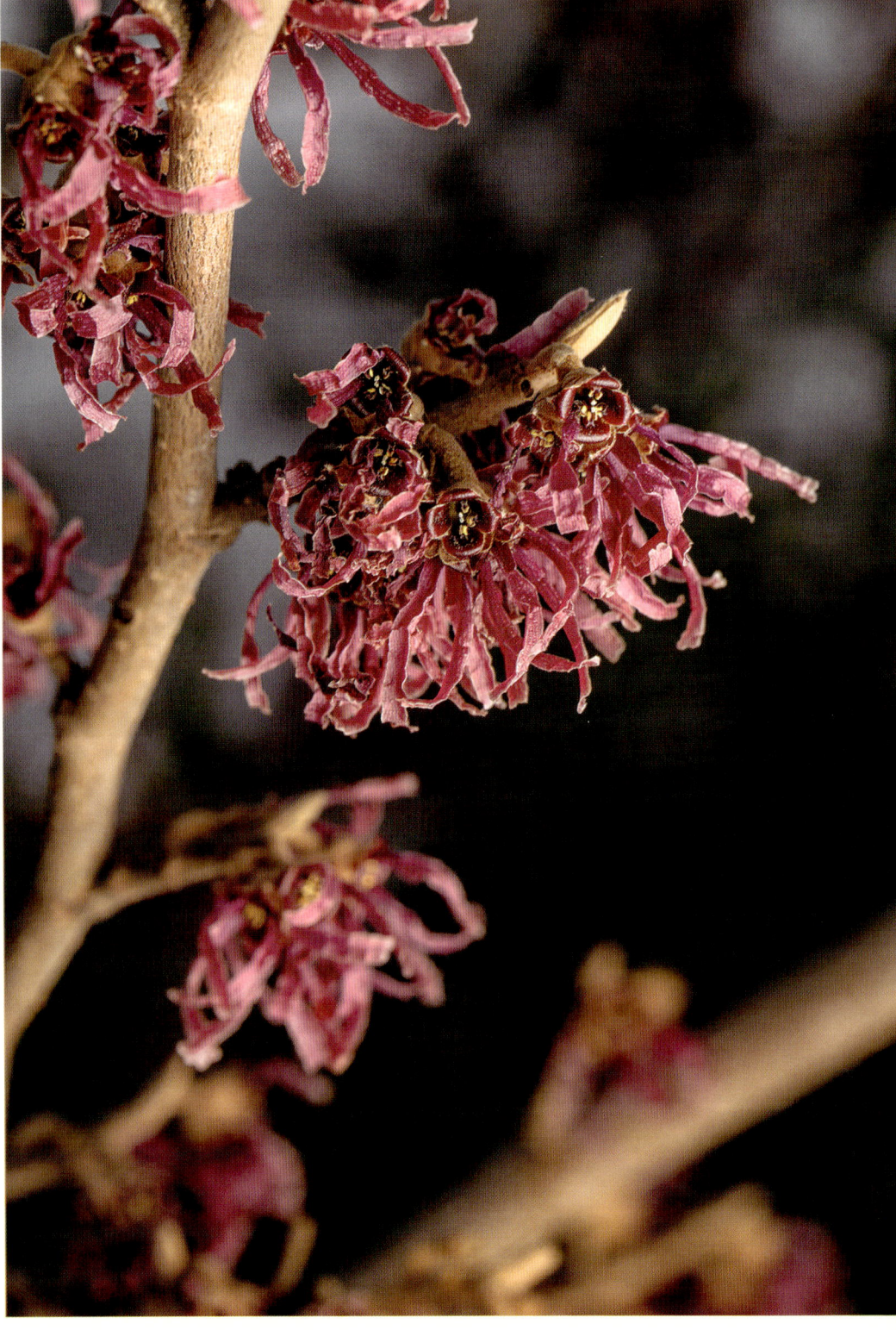

FEBRUARY · MARCH

Witch hazel cultivar (*Hamamelis* × 'Amethyst') Digital image by Hannele Lahti, February 2023
Enid A. Haupt Garden, Washington, DC
Smithsonian Gardens

The brilliant fall color and showy red-to-purple late-winter blooms of *Hamamelis* × 'Amethyst' distinguish it from other witch hazels. A low-maintenance deciduous shrub, it can grow up to ten feet high and loves full sun to partial shade in woodland gardens.

FEBRUARY

S	M	T	W	T	F	S
						1
2	3	4	5	6	7	8
9	10	11	12	13	14	15
16	17	18	19	20	21	22
23	24	25	26	27	28	

MARCH

S	M	T	W	T	F	S
						1
2	3	4	5	6	7	8
9	10	11	12	13	14	15
16	17	18	19	20	21	22
23	24	25	26	27	28	29
30	31					

SUNDAY
23

MONDAY
24

TUESDAY
25

WEDNESDAY
26

● **THURSDAY**
27

RAMADAN BEGINS (SUNDOWN) **FRIDAY**
28

SATURDAY
1

MARCH

SUNDAY
2

MONDAY
3

TUESDAY
4

WEDNESDAY   ASH WEDNESDAY
5

THURSDAY ◐
6

FRIDAY
7

SATURDAY
8

Derek Fordjour (b. 1974)
Birdman, 2022
Acrylic, charcoal, cardboard, oil pastel, and foil on newspaper mounted on canvas
87¾ × 67½ in. (222.9 × 171.5 cm)
Gift of Iris and Adam Singer
Hirshhorn Museum and Sculpture Garden

Memphis-born Derek Fordjour is best known for his vigorously process-oriented approach to painting. *Birdman* is part of a series the artist began in 2020 after reading the fantastical memoir of early twentieth-century magician Black Herman, whose performance, deception, and hustle inspired this circus-themed painting, composed, like many of Fordjour's works, upon a canvas wrapped and layered with cardboard, foil, and copies of the *Financial Times*.

MARCH

S	M	T	W	T	F	S
						1
2	3	4	5	6	7	8
9	10	11	12	13	14	15
16	17	18	19	20	21	22
23	24	25	26	27	28	29
30	31					

APRIL

S	M	T	W	T	F	S
		1	2	3	4	5
6	7	8	9	10	11	12
13	14	15	16	17	18	19
20	21	22	23	24	25	26
27	28	29	30			

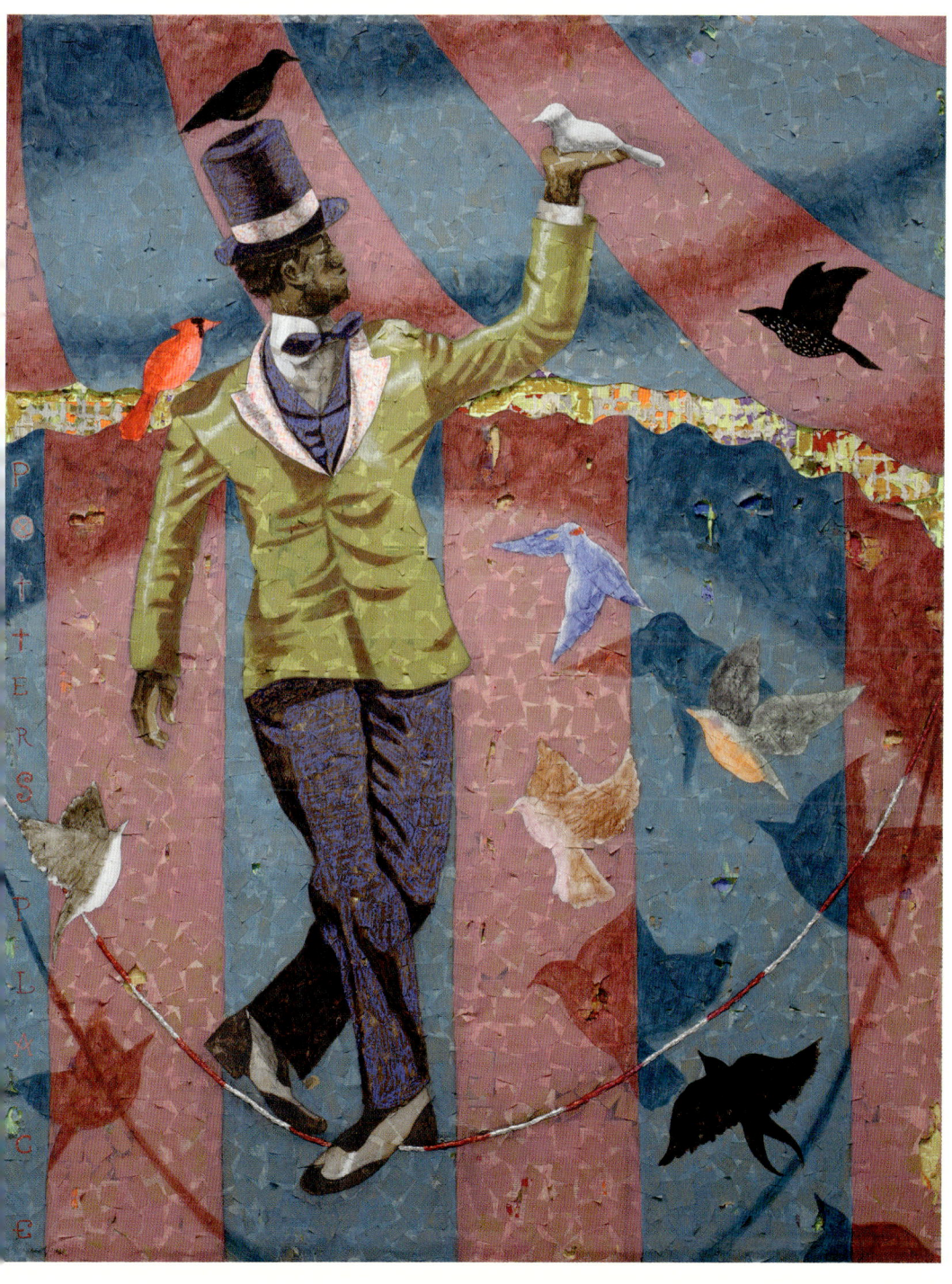

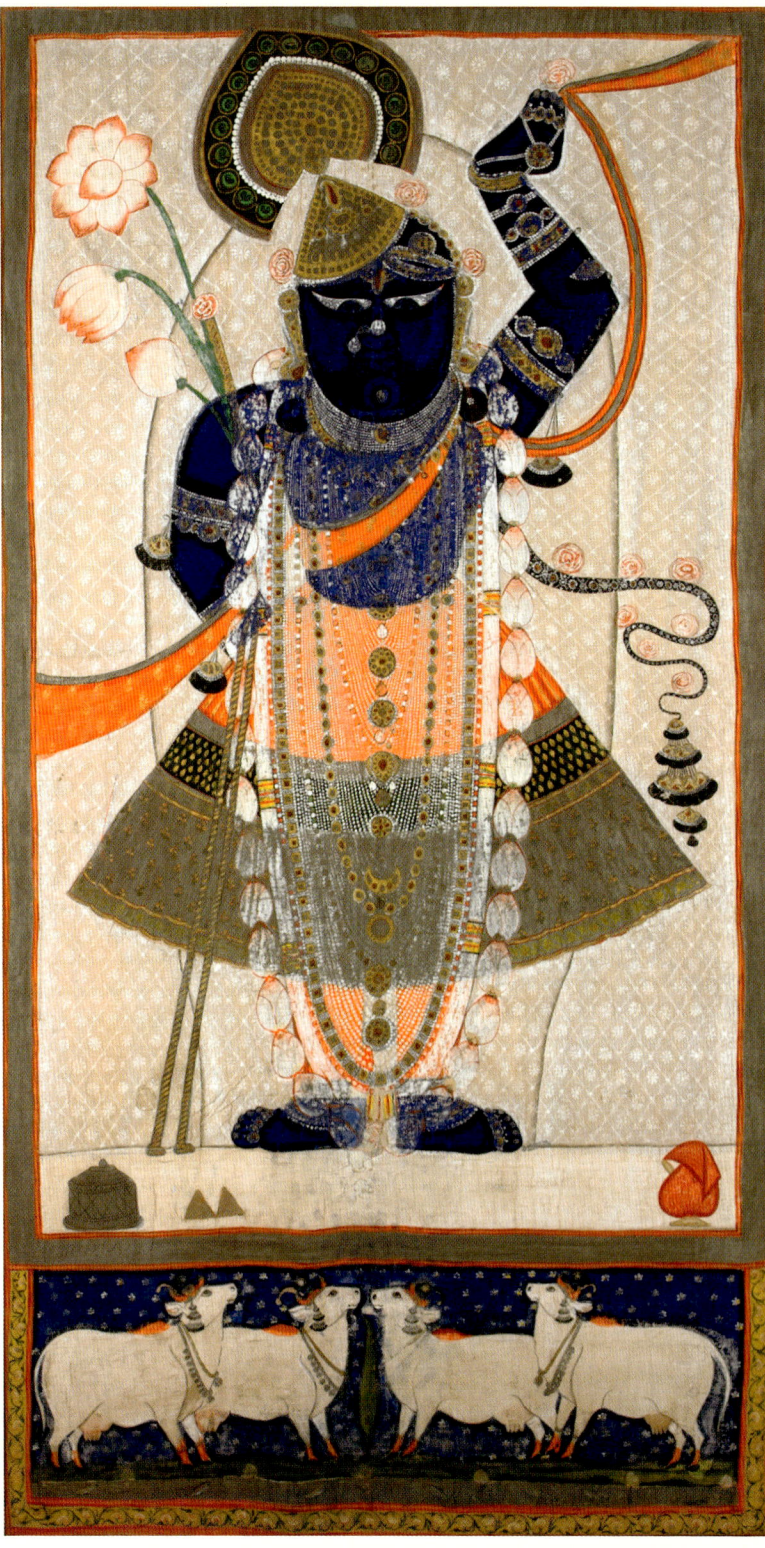

MARCH

Krishna as Sri Nath-ji, India
Opaque watercolor on cotton on stretcher
71⅝ × 37 1/16 in. (182 × 94.2 cm)
Gift of Karl B. Mann
National Museum of Asian Art

When the Hindu god Krishna took human form to live in a rural village, both the cows and their herders became his devotees. This six-foot-high painting represents Krishna as an adorable child with blue skin, lotus-shaped eyes, and a hand raised in a powerfully protective gesture. White cows gaze lovingly at the child-god.

MARCH
S	M	T	W	T	F	S
						1
2	3	4	5	6	7	8
9	10	11	12	13	14	15
16	17	18	19	20	21	22
23	24	25	26	27	28	29
30	31					

APRIL
S	M	T	W	T	F	S
		1	2	3	4	5
6	7	8	9	10	11	12
13	14	15	16	17	18	19
20	21	22	23	24	25	26
27	28	29	30			

DAYLIGHT SAVING TIME BEGINS

SUNDAY 9

MONDAY 10

TUESDAY 11

WEDNESDAY 12

THURSDAY 13

○ HOLI

FRIDAY 14

SATURDAY 15

MARCH

SUNDAY
16

MONDAY   ST. PATRICK'S DAY
17

TUESDAY
18

WEDNESDAY
19

THURSDAY   FIRST DAY OF SPRING
20

FRIDAY
21

SATURDAY ◐
22

Truman Lowe
(Ho-Chunk, 1944–2019)
Sauninga Series, Blue, 1992
Pastel on paper
30 × 22½ in. (76.2 × 56 cm)
National Museum
of the American Indian

Truman Lowe titled his series of pastel drawings depicting bears *Sauninga*, or "Shining One," after his mother, whose name was derived from the Ho-Chunk tribe's Bear Clan. In his hands, the creatures resemble bearskin rugs that are transformed into fantastical flying beings. Lowe is the subject of a retrospective opening at the National Museum of the American Indian in fall 2025.

MARCH

S	M	T	W	T	F	S
						1
2	3	4	5	6	7	8
9	10	11	12	13	14	15
16	17	18	19	20	21	22
23	24	25	26	27	28	29
30	31					

APRIL

S	M	T	W	T	F	S
		1	2	3	4	5
6	7	8	9	10	11	12
13	14	15	16	17	18	19
20	21	22	23	24	25	26
27	28	29	30			

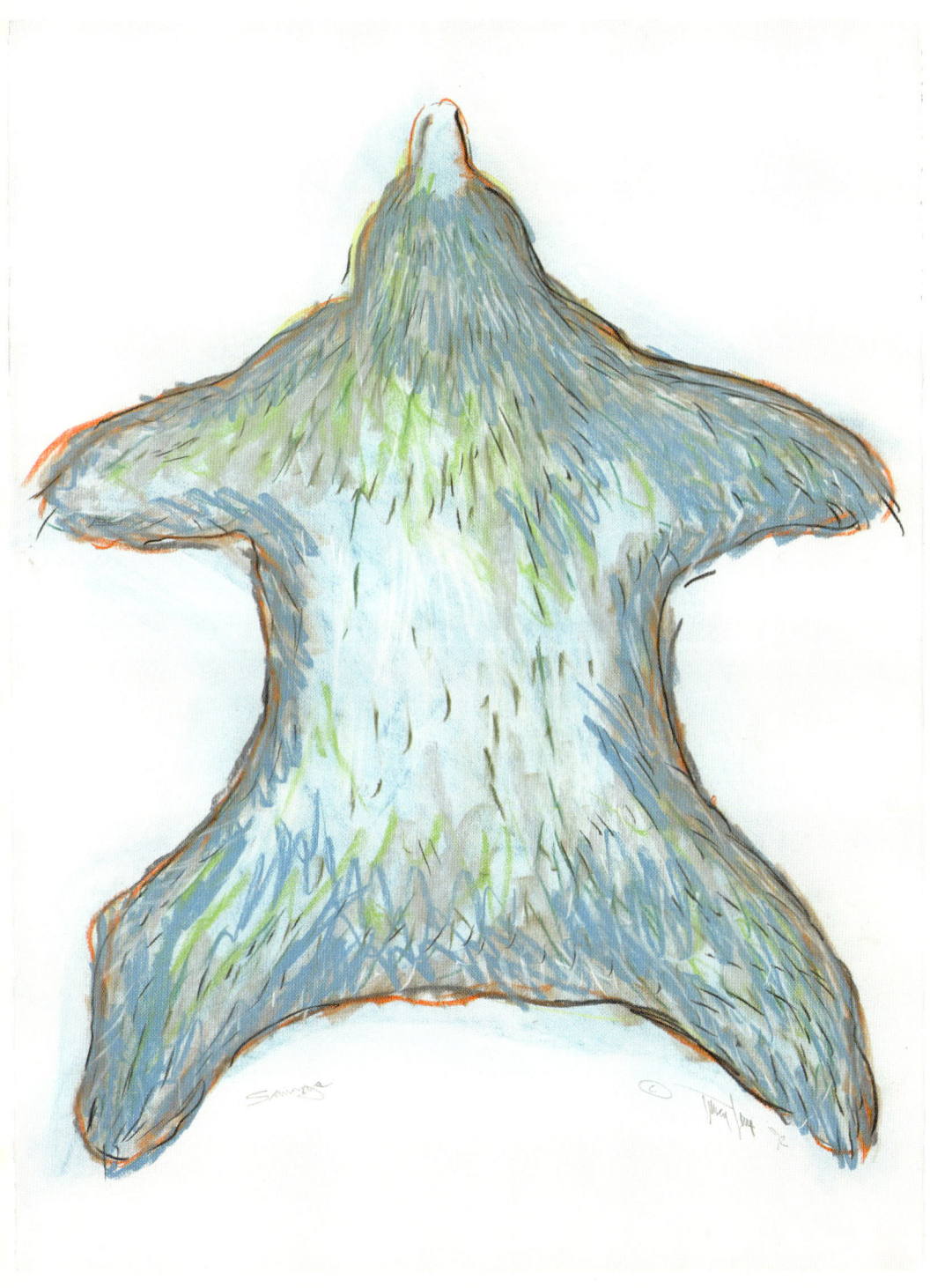

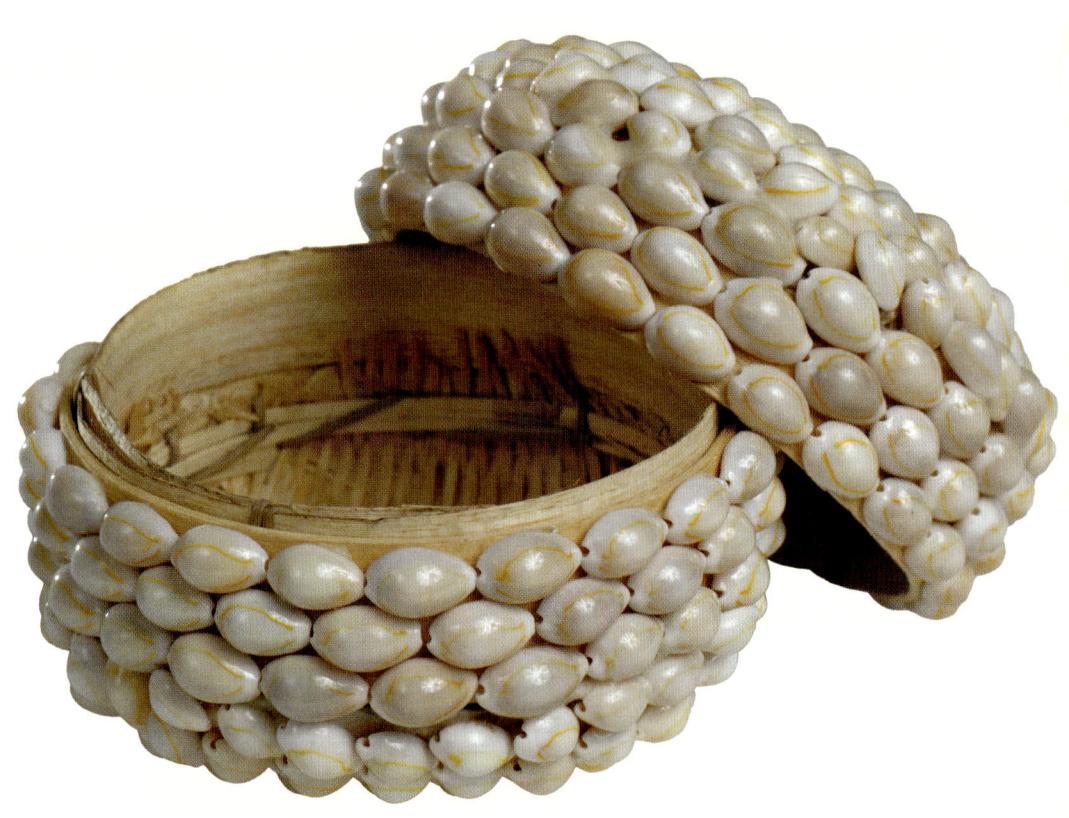

MARCH

Ceremonial basket adorned with cowrie shells, 2015
Mossuril, Mozambique
Fiber and cowrie shell
5⅝ × 6½ × 6½ in.
(14.3 × 16.5 × 16.5 cm)
National Museum of African American History and Culture

In 1794 the owners of the slave ship *São José* enslaved and trafficked 512 people from Mozambique. Half of the captives died when the vessel was wrecked off the coast of Cape Town, and the survivors were sold into slavery in South Africa. Soil from their homeland was carried in this basket and deposited at the site of the shipwreck in 2015.

MARCH

S	M	T	W	T	F	S
						1
2	3	4	5	6	7	8
9	10	11	12	13	14	15
16	17	18	19	20	21	22
23	24	25	26	27	28	29
30	31					

APRIL

S	M	T	W	T	F	S
		1	2	3	4	5
6	7	8	9	10	11	12
13	14	15	16	17	18	19
20	21	22	23	24	25	26
27	28	29	30			

SUNDAY 23

MONDAY 24

TUESDAY 25

WEDNESDAY 26

THURSDAY 27

FRIDAY 28

● RAMADAN ENDS (SUNDOWN)

SATURDAY 29

MARCH · APRIL

SUNDAY
30

MONDAY
31

TUESDAY
1

WEDNESDAY
2

THURSDAY
3

FRIDAY
4

SATURDAY
5

James Presley Ball
(1825–1904)
Unidentified sitters,
c. 1853–58
Half-plate daguerreotype
L. J. West Collection
of Early African American
Photography
Smithsonian American
Art Museum

While daguerreotypes, the earliest form of photography, were more affordable than painted portraits, they were not as accessible to all classes as later, less expensive forms of photography. The refined nature of this family's self-presentation, especially the silk dress and the jewelry worn by the mother, shows the wealth of the clientele that James Presley Ball, a prominent African American photographer and abolitionist, served.

MARCH
S	M	T	W	T	F	S
						1
2	3	4	5	6	7	8
9	10	11	12	13	14	15
16	17	18	19	20	21	22
23	24	25	26	27	28	29
30	31					

APRIL
S	M	T	W	T	F	S
		1	2	3	4	5
6	7	8	9	10	11	12
13	14	15	16	17	18	19
20	21	22	23	24	25	26
27	28	29	30			

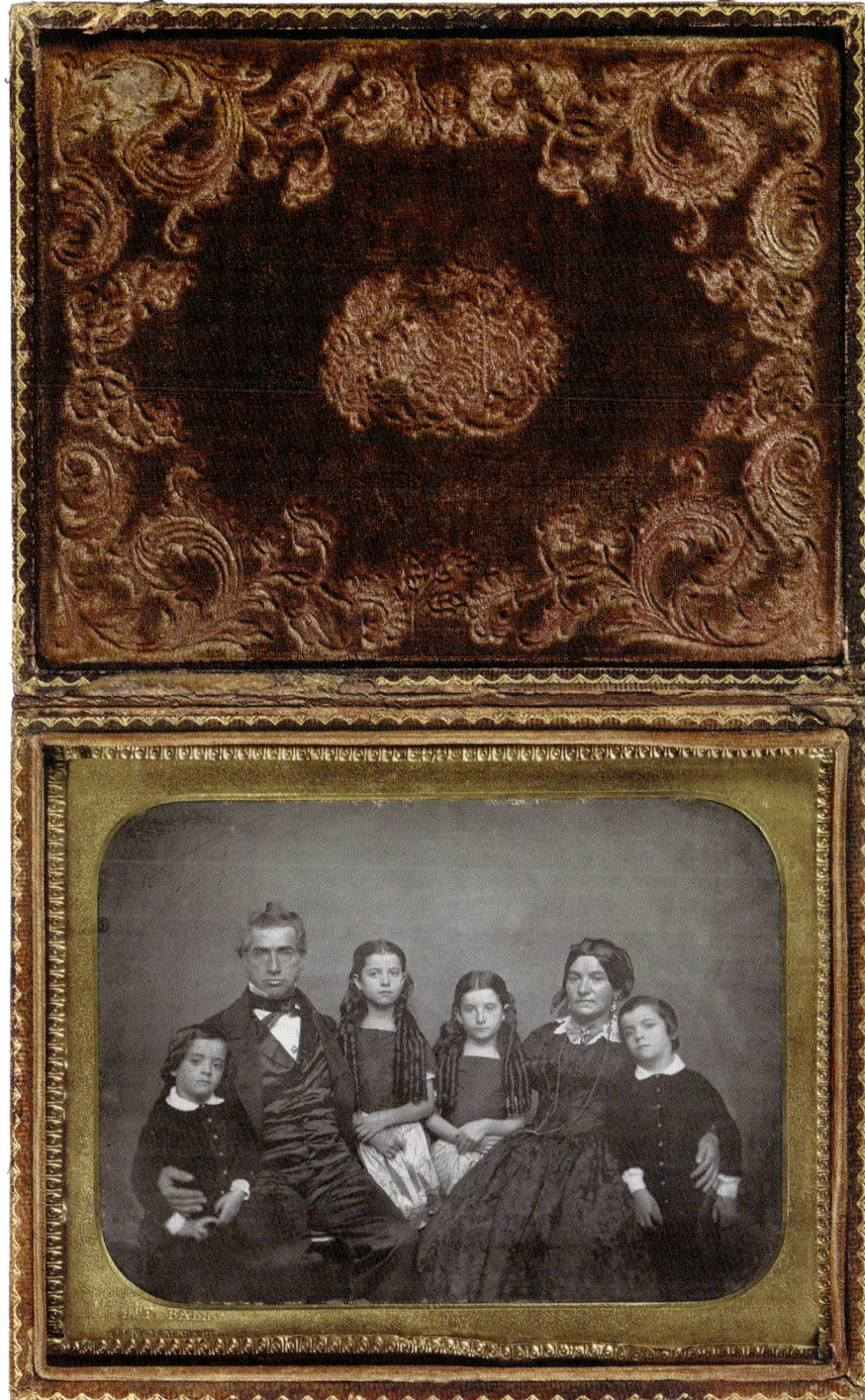

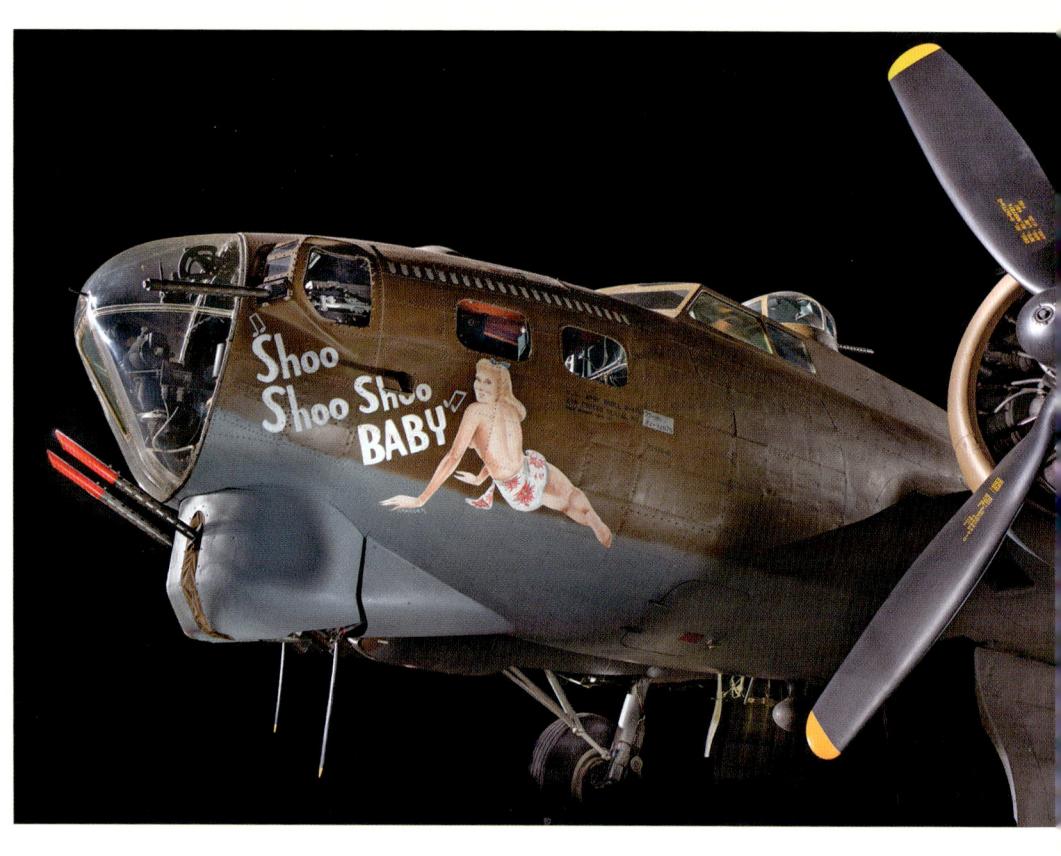

Shoo Shoo Shoo Baby B-17
Flying Fortress, 1944
Manufactured by Boeing,
Seattle, WA
Aluminum and steel
Span: 103 ft. 10 in. (31.6 m)
Length: 74 ft. 4 in. (22.6 m)
Height: 19 ft. 1 in. (5.8 m)
National Air
and Space Museum

Shoo Shoo Shoo Baby is one of the most significant remaining World War II B-17 bombers. Named for a popular Andrews Sisters song, it flew twenty-four missions over Europe during the war. The plane is planned to go on display in 2025 at the Steven F. Udvar-Hazy Center in Chantilly, VA.

APRIL

S	M	T	W	T	F	S
		1	2	3	4	5
6	7	8	9	10	11	12
13	14	15	16	17	18	19
20	21	22	23	24	25	26
27	28	29	30			

MAY

S	M	T	W	T	F	S
				1	2	3
4	5	6	7	8	9	10
11	12	13	14	15	16	17
18	19	20	21	22	23	24
25	26	27	28	29	30	31

APRIL

SUNDAY
6

MONDAY
7

TUESDAY
8

WEDNESDAY
9

THURSDAY
10

FRIDAY
11

○ PASSOVER BEGINS (SUNDOWN)

SATURDAY
12

APRIL

SUNDAY   PALM SUNDAY

13

MONDAY

14

TUESDAY

15

WEDNESDAY

16

THURSDAY

17

FRIDAY   GOOD FRIDAY

18

SATURDAY

19

Nanae Momiyama
(1924–2002)
Flower Sketch, n.d.
Various media
10½ × 9½ in. (27 × 24 cm)
Nanae Momiyama papers,
1928–c. 2000
Archives of American Art

While Japanese American artist and educator Nanae Momiyama was an expert in traditional Japanese calligraphy and sumi-e painting, yet her style extended to abstract expressionism and design for film and theater posters. She always rooted her work in the natural world, writing: "As far back as I remember, Nature—from tiny insects to mighty trees—has always been my true source of inspiration."

```
              APRIL
S   M   T   W   T   F   S
            1   2   3   4   5
6   7   8   9  10  11  12
13  14  15  16  17  18  19
20  21  22  23  24  25  26
27  28  29  30

               MAY
S   M   T   W   T   F   S
                    1   2   3
4   5   6   7   8   9  10
11  12  13  14  15  16  17
18  19  20  21  22  23  24
25  26  27  28  29  30  31
```

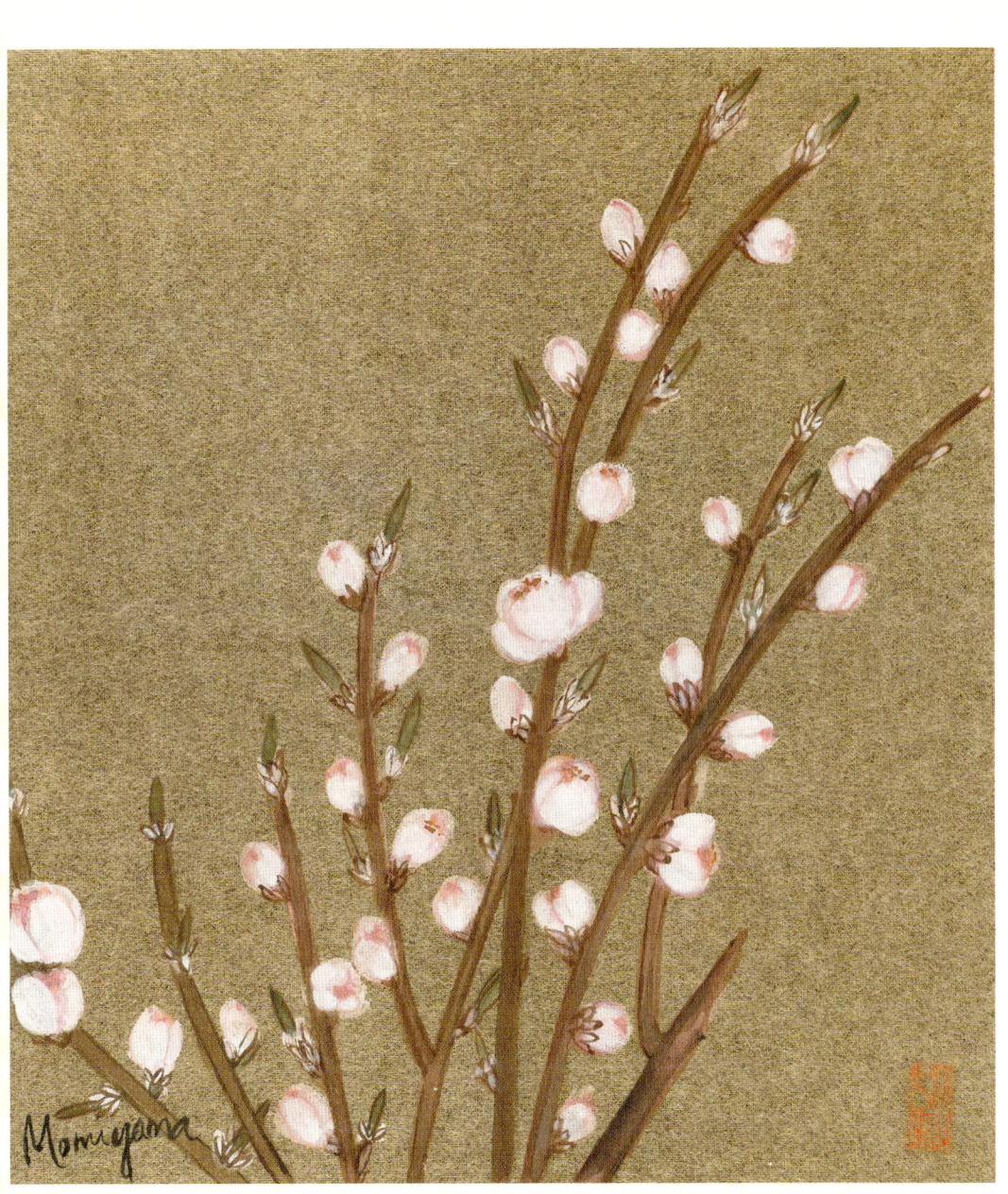

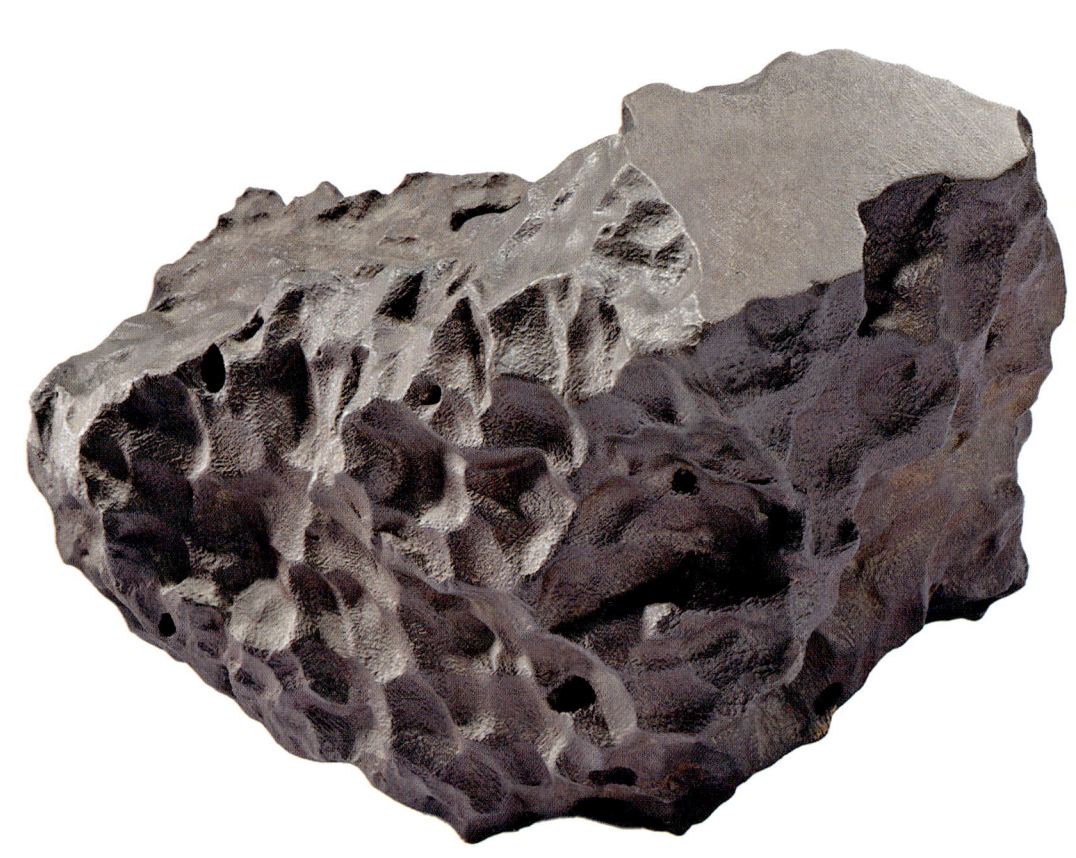

APRIL

Drum Mountains meteorite
Millard County, UT
1,164 lbs. (528 kg)
National Museum of Natural History

The Drum Mountains meteorite was discovered in 1944 by Akio Ujihara and Yoshio Nishimoto near the Central Utah Relocation Center (Topaz) Site in Utah, where both were interned during World War II. Desert sand has eroded the meteorite's surface, revealing its internal crosshatch-like Widmanstätten pattern. Visitors can see this IIIAB iron meteorite in the Janet Annenberg Hooker Hall of Geology, Gems, and Minerals in the National Museum of Natural History.

☽ EASTER · ORTHODOX EASTER
PASSOVER ENDS (SUNDOWN)

SUNDAY
20

EASTER MONDAY (CAN.)

MONDAY
21

EARTH DAY

TUESDAY
22

WEDNESDAY
23

THURSDAY
24

FRIDAY
25

SATURDAY
26

APRIL
S	M	T	W	T	F	S
		1	2	3	4	5
6	7	8	9	10	11	12
13	14	15	16	17	18	19
20	21	22	23	24	25	26
27	28	29	30			

MAY
S	M	T	W	T	F	S
				1	2	3
4	5	6	7	8	9	10
11	12	13	14	15	16	17
18	19	20	21	22	23	24
25	26	27	28	29	30	31

APRIL · MAY

SUNDAY
27

MONDAY
28

TUESDAY
29

WEDNESDAY
30

THURSDAY
1

FRIDAY
2

SATURDAY
3

Lisa Holt (Cochiti Pueblo, b. 1980) and Harlan Reano (Santo Domingo/Kewa Pueblo, b. 1978)
Standing singing rabbit, 2023
Cochiti, Santo Domingo, NM
Ceramic pottery
20¼ × 10¾ × 4¼ in. (51 × 27 × 11 cm)
Smithsonian Craft Show

Artists Lisa Holt and Harlan Reano were inspired by childhood hunts with family members along with other tribal members in the hills of Santo Domingo and Cochiti Pueblo. In hunting, sometimes the animal is caught, and sometimes it isn't. This artwork depicts the celebration of a rabbit that escaped capture.

APRIL
S	M	T	W	T	F	S
		1	2	3	4	5
6	7	8	9	10	11	12
13	14	15	16	17	18	19
20	21	22	23	24	25	26
27	28	29	30			

MAY
S	M	T	W	T	F	S
				1	2	3
4	5	6	7	8	9	10
11	12	13	14	15	16	17
18	19	20	21	22	23	24
25	26	27	28	29	30	31

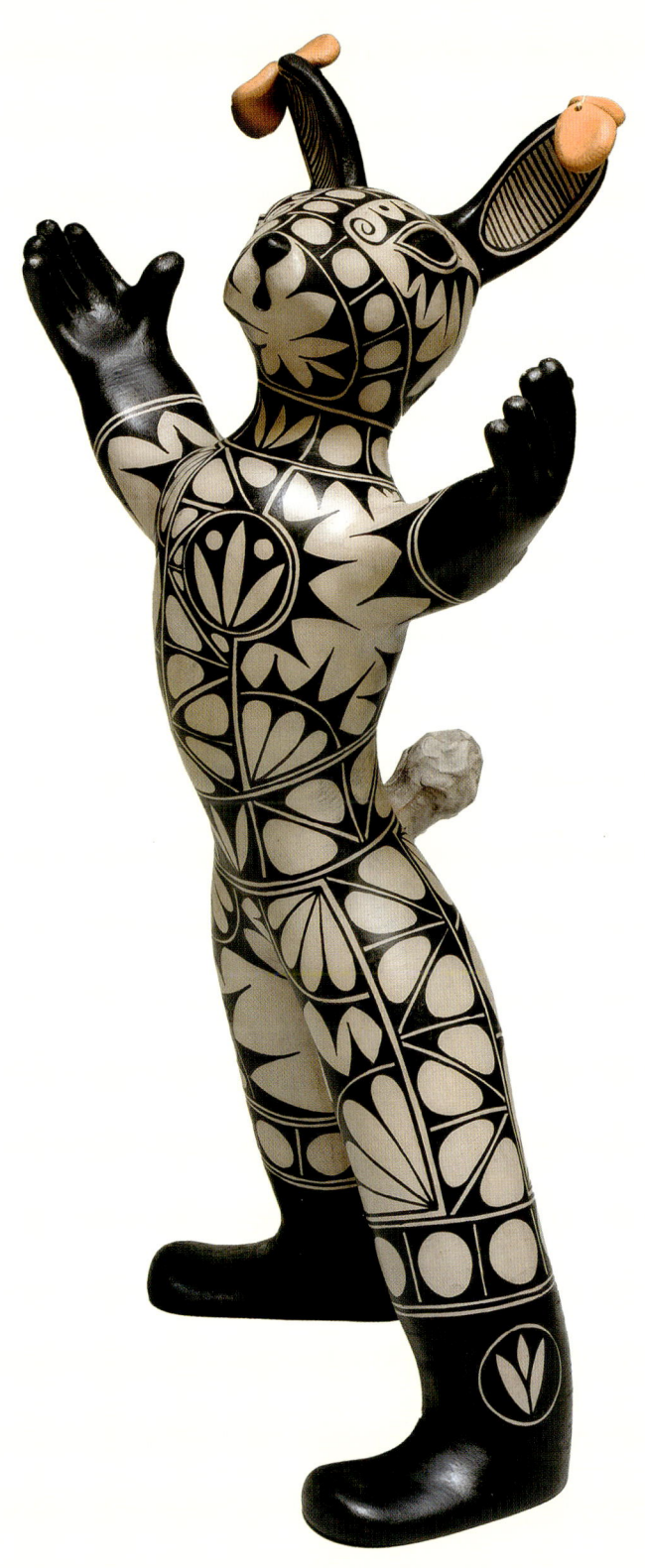

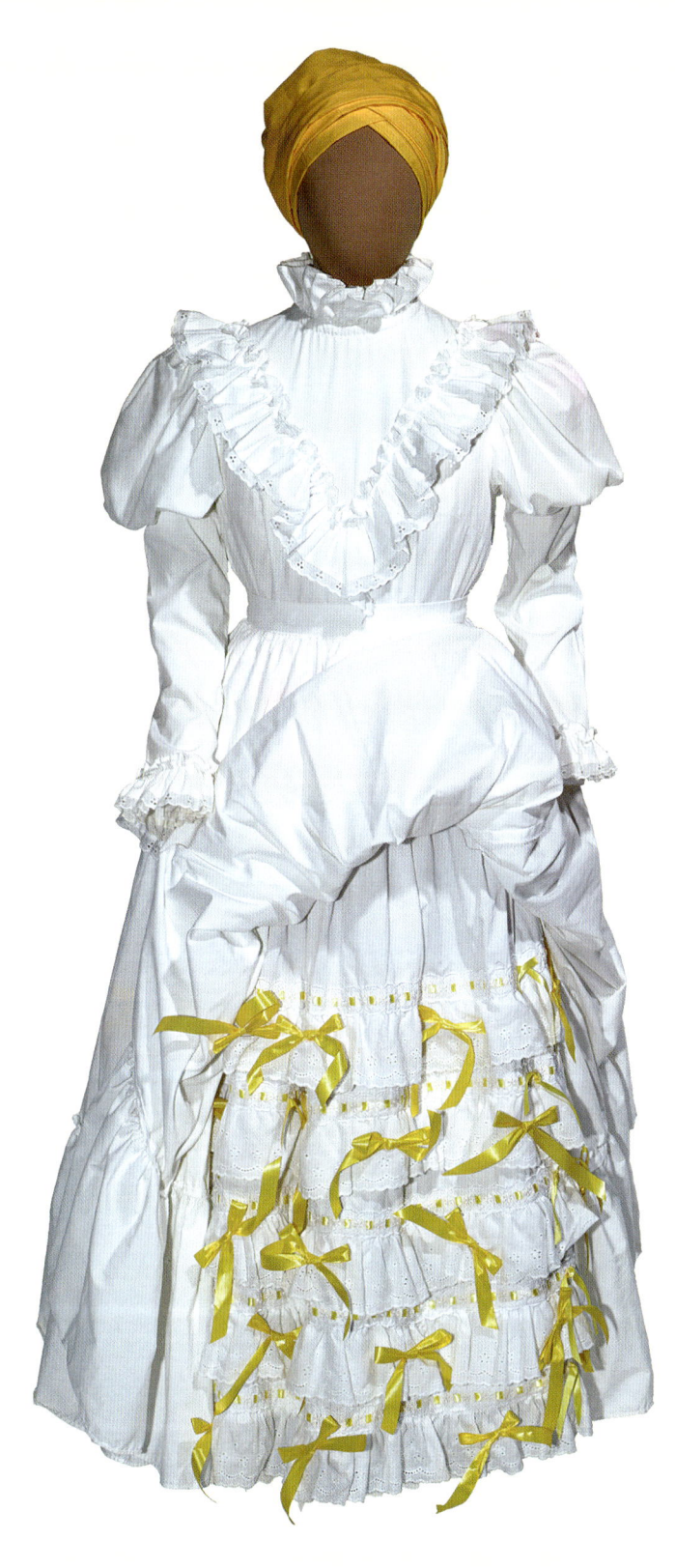

MAY

Bomba performance outfit worn by Margarita "Tata" Cepeda, n.d.
Puerto Rico
Fabric
57 × 19½ in. (144.8 × 49.5 cm)
Gift of Margarita Sánchez Cepeda
National Museum of American History

Brought to Puerto Rico by enslaved West Africans, bomba is a dance of resistance as much as of joy. Because the music's rhythmic drumming follows the movements of the dancer, bomba has long been used to communicate defiance that would have been policed if spoken. Margarita "Tata" Cepeda (b. 1962) comes from a family steeped in bomba. Her grandmother Caridad "Mami Cari" Brenes Caballero (1916–1994) drew from traditional Afro–Puerto Rican fashions for this bomba dress, including the use of a pañuelo (headscarf).

MAY
S	M	T	W	T	F	S
				1	2	3
4	5	6	7	8	9	10
11	12	13	14	15	16	17
18	19	20	21	22	23	24
25	26	27	28	29	30	31

JUNE
S	M	T	W	T	F	S
1	2	3	4	5	6	7
8	9	10	11	12	13	14
15	16	17	18	19	20	21
22	23	24	25	26	27	28
29	30					

SUNDAY
4

MONDAY
5
CINCO DE MAYO

TUESDAY
6

WEDNESDAY
7

THURSDAY
8

FRIDAY
9

SATURDAY
10

MAY

SUNDAY	MOTHER'S DAY
11	

MONDAY
12 ○

TUESDAY
13

WEDNESDAY
14

THURSDAY
15

FRIDAY
16

SATURDAY
17

Julia Chon
I Gave a Lot of Water to My Flower of Laughter, 2022
Acrylic paint on earthenware *onggi danji* jar
11 × 10 1/16 in. (28 × 25.5 cm)
Gift of the David and Julie Chon Family
Anacostia Community Museum

DC-area artist Julia Chon, also known as Kimchi Juice, here uses a traditional Korean earthenware jar as a canvas for a vibrant floral motif. Her work explores the relationship between cultural tradition and generational identity in the Korean diaspora. The *onggi* pot is typically used to store fermented sauces and is often passed down from generation to generation, while yellow chrysanthemums are used in funerary ceremonies in Korea, where they symbolize the cycle of life.

MAY
S	M	T	W	T	F	S
				1	2	3
4	5	6	7	8	9	10
11	12	13	14	15	16	17
18	19	20	21	22	23	24
25	26	27	28	29	30	31

JUNE
S	M	T	W	T	F	S
1	2	3	4	5	6	7
8	9	10	11	12	13	14
15	16	17	18	19	20	21
22	23	24	25	26	27	28
29	30					

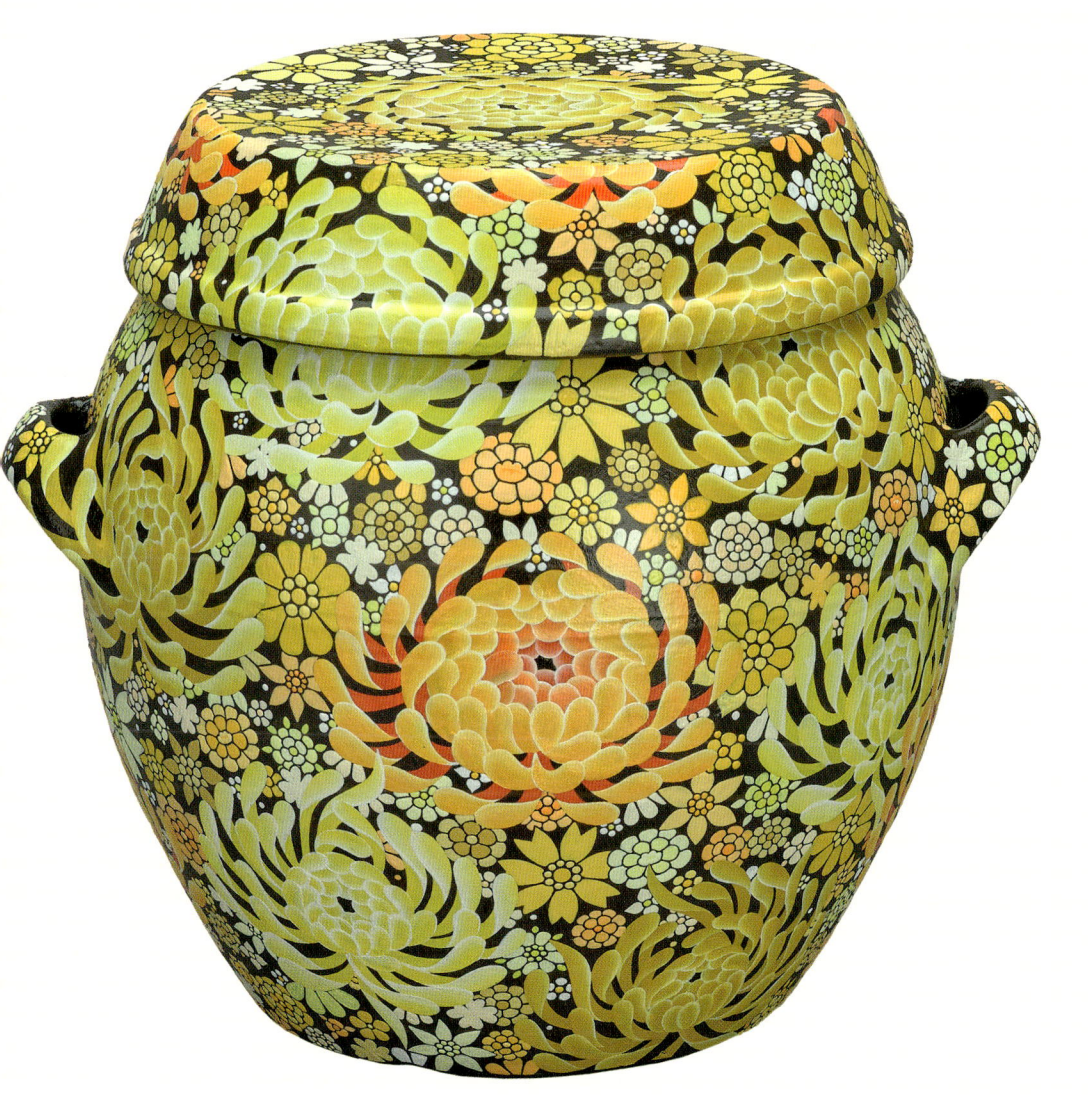

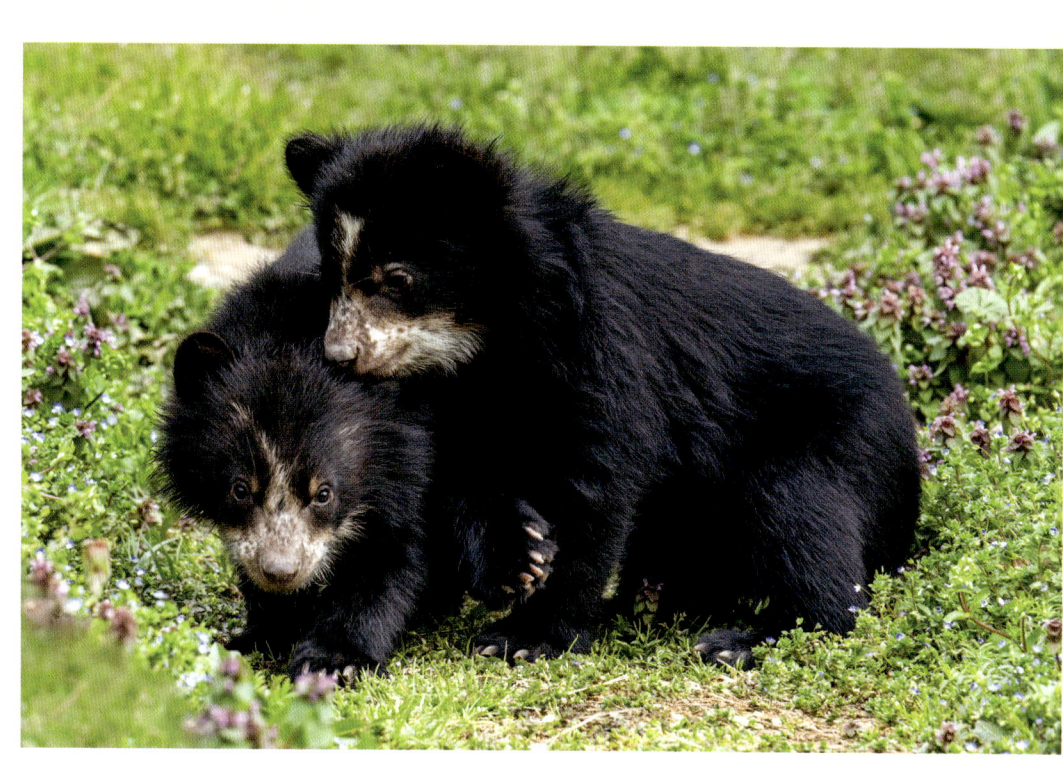

MAY

Andean bear (*Tremarctos ornatus*)
Digital photograph by Roshan Patel,
March 22, 2023
Washington, DC
Smithsonian's National Zoo and Conservation Biology Institute

Ever since rambunctious Andean bear brothers Ian and Sean were born November 15, 2022, they have delighted visitors by exploring, tussling, and tumbling around their habitat. The Smithsonian's National Zoo and Conservation Biology Institute works with accredited zoos around the world to coordinate breeding to ensure genetic diversity for the long-term survival of this charismatic species.

MAY
S	M	T	W	T	F	S
				1	2	3
4	5	6	7	8	9	10
11	12	13	14	15	16	17
18	19	20	21	22	23	24
25	26	27	28	29	30	31

JUNE
S	M	T	W	T	F	S
1	2	3	4	5	6	7
8	9	10	11	12	13	14
15	16	17	18	19	20	21
22	23	24	25	26	27	28
29	30					

SUNDAY 18

MONDAY 19 — VICTORIA DAY (CAN.)

TUESDAY 20

WEDNESDAY 21

THURSDAY 22

FRIDAY 23

SATURDAY 24

MAY

SUNDAY
25

MONDAY   MEMORIAL DAY ●
26

TUESDAY
27

WEDNESDAY
28

THURSDAY
29

FRIDAY
30

SATURDAY
31

Clara Maass 13¢ stamp, 1976
Designed by Paul Calle (1928–2010)
Paper, ink, adhesive
1 9/16 × 1 1/4 in. (4 × 3.2 cm)
National Postal Museum

Clara Maass (1876–1901) worked as an army nurse in Florida, Cuba, and the Philippines during the Spanish-American War of 1898. In 1900 she returned to Cuba, where she became involved in a study of the cause of yellow fever. To determine whether the tropical fever was caused by city filth or the bite of a mosquito, seven volunteers—including Maass—were bitten by mosquitoes. Two men died, but Maass survived. She volunteered again several months later, this time being infected. Maass died of yellow fever at the age of twenty-five.

MAY

S	M	T	W	T	F	S
				1	2	3
4	5	6	7	8	9	10
11	12	13	14	15	16	17
18	19	20	21	22	23	24
25	26	27	28	29	30	31

JUNE

S	M	T	W	T	F	S
1	2	3	4	5	6	7
8	9	10	11	12	13	14
15	16	17	18	19	20	21
22	23	24	25	26	27	28
29	30					

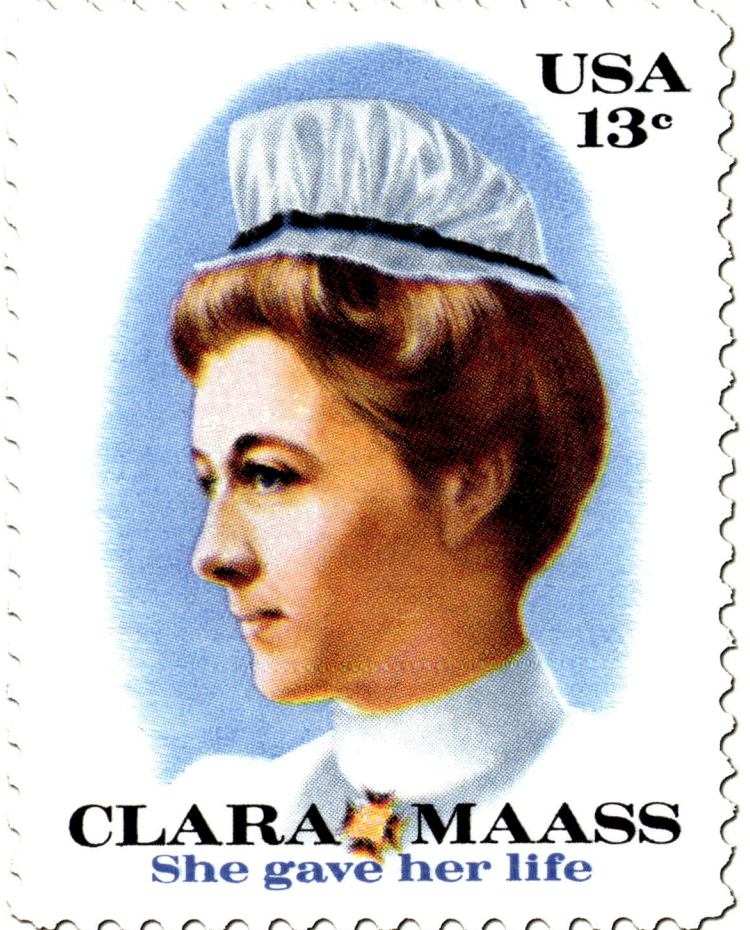

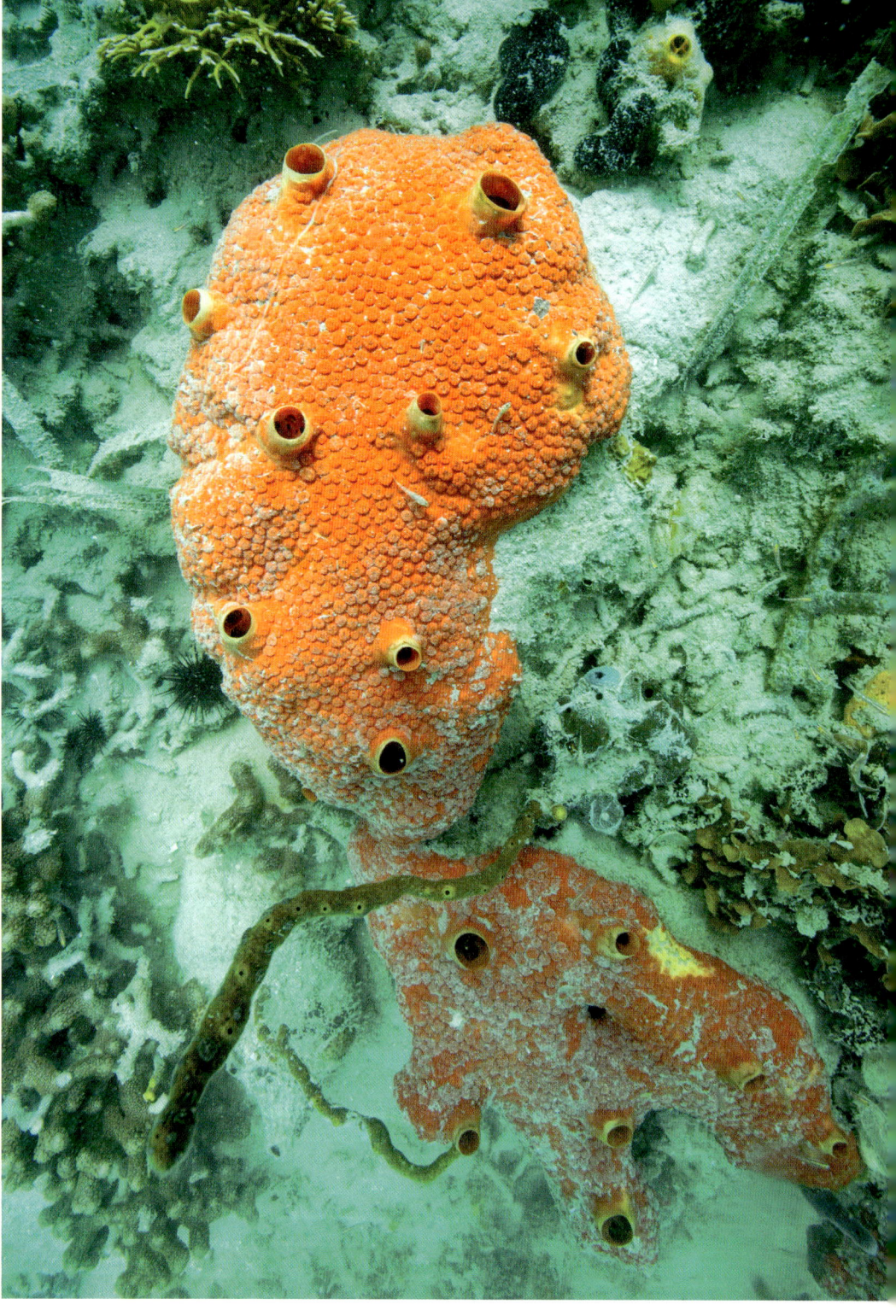

JUNE

Red boring sponge
Digital photography by
Jorge Alemán, July 2019
Bocas del Toro, Panama
Smithsonian Tropical
Research Institute

The red boring sponge (*Cliona delitrix*), photographed near the Smithsonian Tropical Research Institute in Panama, is anything but tedious. Its name comes from its habit of burrowing into the skeletons of dying or dead massive coral reefs in the Caribbean, often contributing to the bioerosion of entire reef colonies.

JUNE

S	M	T	W	T	F	S
1	2	3	4	5	6	7
8	9	10	11	12	13	14
15	16	17	18	19	20	21
22	23	24	25	26	27	28
29	30					

JULY

S	M	T	W	T	F	S
		1	2	3	4	5
6	7	8	9	10	11	12
13	14	15	16	17	18	19
20	21	22	23	24	25	26
27	28	29	30	31		

SUNDAY
1

MONDAY
2

TUESDAY
3

WEDNESDAY
4

THURSDAY
5

EID AL-ADHA BEGINS (SUNDOWN)   **FRIDAY**
6

EID AL-ADHA ENDS (SUNDOWN)   **SATURDAY**
7

JUNE

SUNDAY
8

MONDAY
9

TUESDAY
10

WEDNESDAY ○
11

THURSDAY
12

FRIDAY
13

SATURDAY — FLAG DAY
14

Gay Power newspaper, 1969
New York, NY
Ink, newsprint
17½ × 11½ in
(44.5 × 29.2 cm)
Archives Center Lesbian, Gay, Bisexual, Transgender (LGBT) Collection
National Museum of American History

Gay Power was a short-lived publication featuring the rising and increasingly open gay culture of New York City. This issue was published in December 1969, just three months after the Stonewall Uprising, a series of protests from the gay community in response to a police raid of the Stonewall Inn in Manhattan.

JUNE
S	M	T	W	T	F	S
						1
2	3	4	5	6	7	
8	9	10	11	12	13	14
15	16	17	18	19	20	21
22	23	24	25	26	27	28
29	30					

JULY
S	M	T	W	T	F	S
		1	2	3	4	5
6	7	8	9	10	11	12
13	14	15	16	17	18	19
20	21	22	23	24	25	26
27	28	29	30	31		

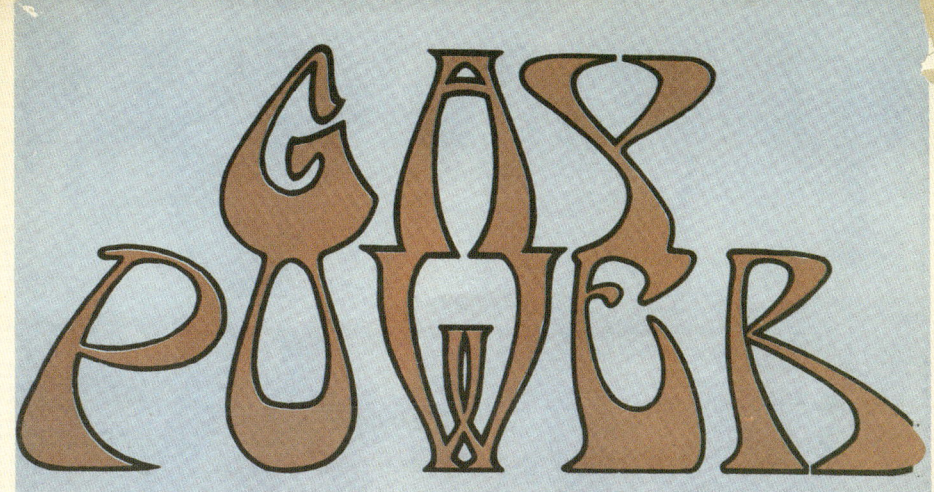

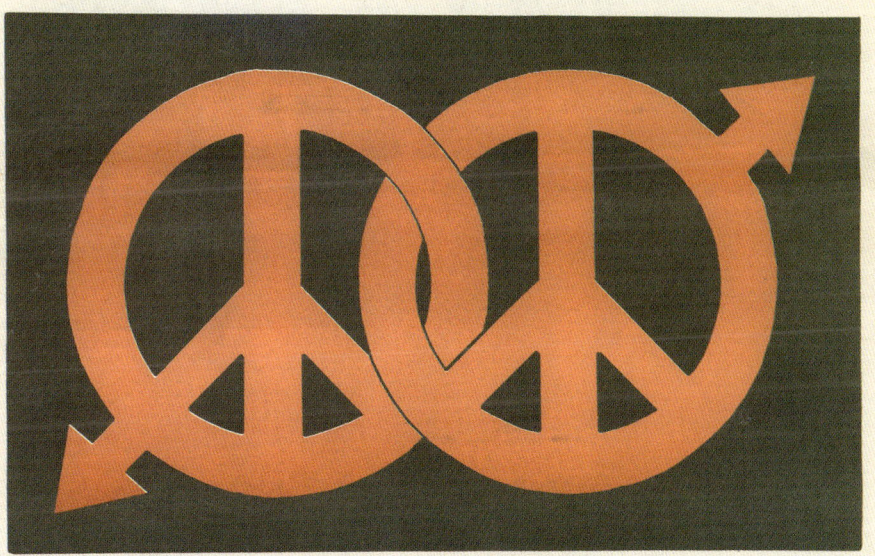

VOLUME 1 #1

PRICE 35¢
Out Of Town 75¢

Floras profile

Floras profile
Flora

JUNE

Hand-cut silhouette of Flora, a woman enslaved in Connecticut, c. 1796
Stratford, CT
Wove paper on millboard
14 × 13 in. (35.6 × 33 cm)
National Museum of African American History and Culture
National Portrait Gallery

Flora's haunting image leaves us wondering about the enslaved woman's life and the circumstances around her portrait. Was she forced to sit for the silhouette? Did she have control of her image? Records show that Asa Benjamin purchased Flora from a woman enslaver. This rare portrait depicts both the sitter's humanity and the inhumanity of slavery.

JUNE

S	M	T	W	T	F	S
1	2	3	4	5	6	7
8	9	10	11	12	13	14
15	16	17	18	19	20	21
22	23	24	25	26	27	28
29	30					

JULY

S	M	T	W	T	F	S
		1	2	3	4	5
6	7	8	9	10	11	12
13	14	15	16	17	18	19
20	21	22	23	24	25	26
27	28	29	30	31		

FATHER'S DAY

SUNDAY
15

MONDAY
16

TUESDAY
17

◐ **WEDNESDAY**
18

JUNETEENTH

THURSDAY
19

FIRST DAY OF SUMMER

FRIDAY
20

SATURDAY
21

JUNE

SUNDAY
22

MONDAY
23

TUESDAY
24

WEDNESDAY ●
25

THURSDAY   MUHARRAM BEGINS (SUNDOWN)
26

FRIDAY
27

SATURDAY
28

Aerialist Emma Grace Clarke, age eleven, performs with Sailor Circus at the 2017 Smithsonian Folklife Festival
Digital photograph by Daniel Martinez Gonzalez, 2017
Washington, DC
Smithsonian Center for Folklife and Cultural Heritage

In the majestic rotunda of the Smithsonian's Arts and Industries Building, young performers at the 2017 Smithsonian Folklife Festival soared on silks and displayed a bright future for the circus arts. Youth culture more broadly will be the festival's primary theme in 2025.

JUNE
S	M	T	W	T	F	S
						1
2	3	4	5	6	7	8
9	10	11	12	13	14	15
16	17	18	19	20	21	22
23	24	25	26	27	28	29
30						

JULY
S	M	T	W	T	F	S
		1	2	3	4	5
6	7	8	9	10	11	12
13	14	15	16	17	18	19
20	21	22	23	24	25	26
27	28	29	30	31		

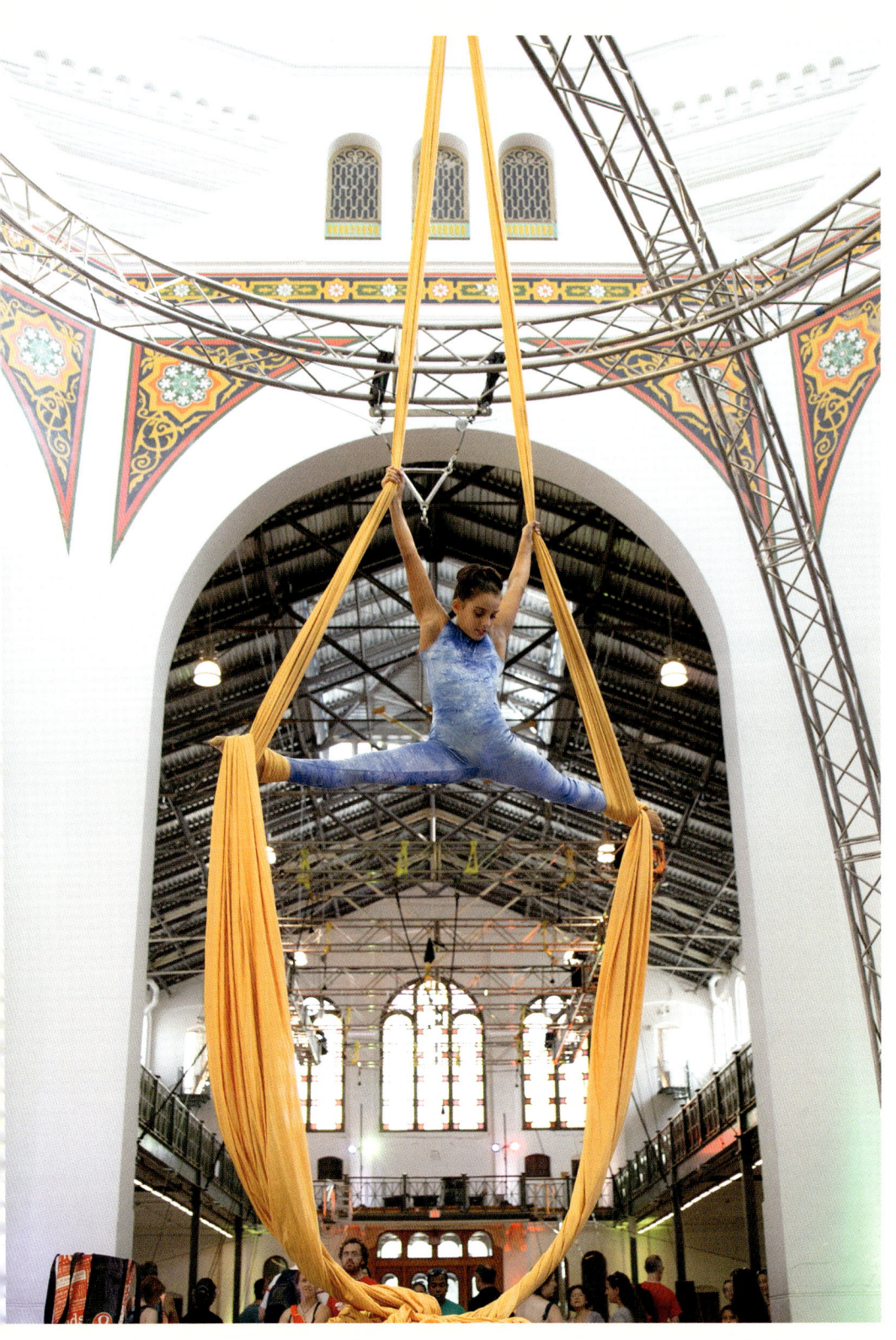

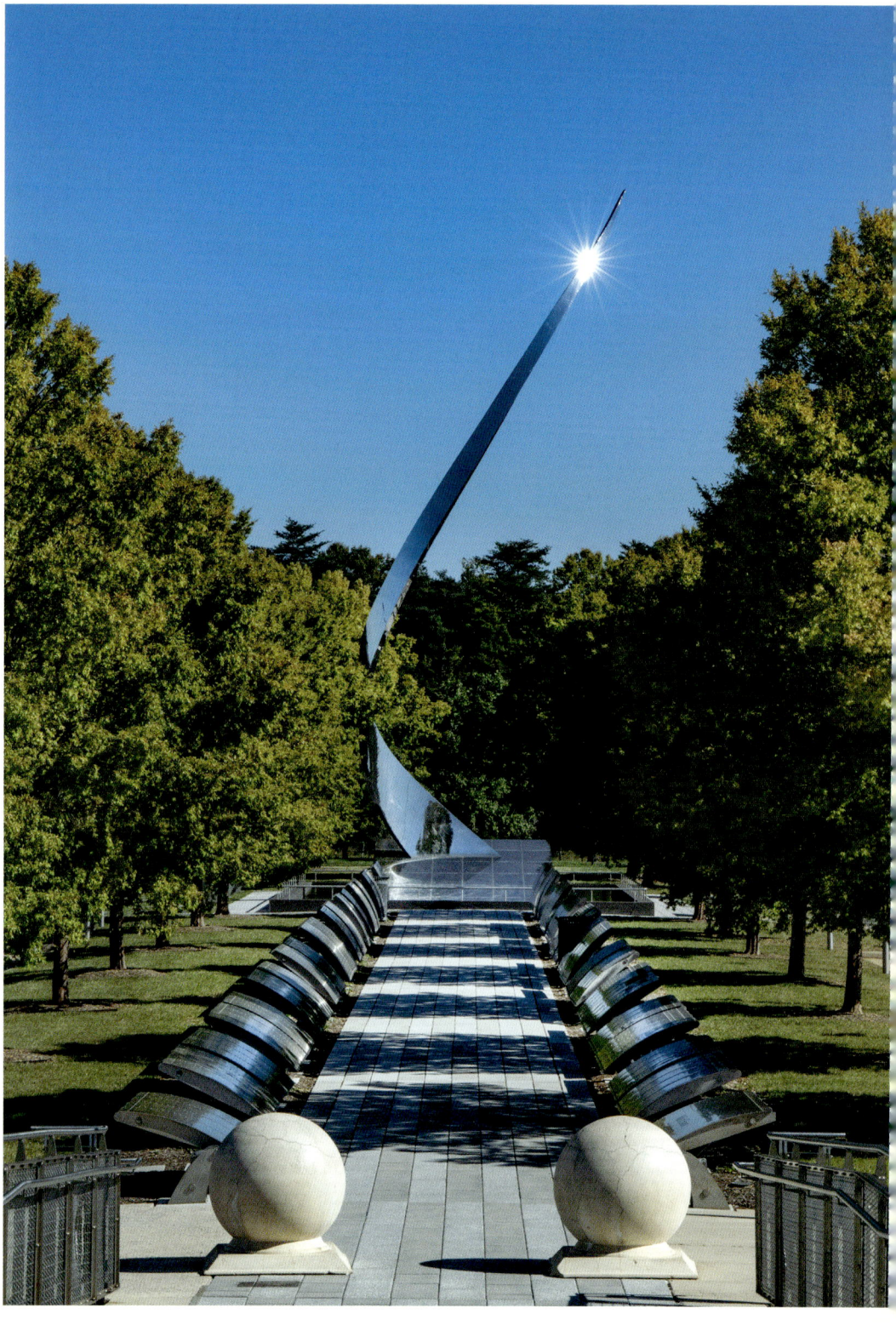

JUNE · JULY

Ascent sculpture
and the Wall of Honor
Digital photo by
Jim Preston, October 2021
Chantilly, VA
Steven F. Udvar-Hazy Center
National Air and Space Museum

The 70-foot tall *Ascent* sculpture was created and donated by Virginia artist John Safer (1922–2018) to commemorate the human journey of flight. It sits outside the Steven F. Udvar-Hazy Center at the end of the Wall of Honor, a permanent memorial that recognizes people with a passion for flight.

JUNE
S	M	T	W	T	F	S
1	2	3	4	5	6	7
8	9	10	11	12	13	14
15	16	17	18	19	20	21
22	23	24	25	26	27	28
29	30					

JULY
S	M	T	W	T	F	S
		1	2	3	4	5
6	7	8	9	10	11	12
13	14	15	16	17	18	19
20	21	22	23	24	25	26
27	28	29	30	31		

SUNDAY 29

MONDAY 30

CANADA DAY — **TUESDAY 1**

WEDNESDAY 2

THURSDAY 3

INDEPENDENCE DAY — **FRIDAY 4**

SATURDAY 5

JULY

SUNDAY
6

MONDAY
7

TUESDAY
8

WEDNESDAY
9

THURSDAY
10

FRIDAY
11

SATURDAY
12

George Peter Alexander Healy (1813–1894)
Delia Spencer Caton Field, 1876
Oil on canvas
48 × 36 in. (122 × 91.5 cm)
Gift of Albert and Maddy Beveridge
National Portrait Gallery

Known for her philanthropy, Delia Spencer Caton Field (1853–1937) was an organizer of the Pure Food Movement in Chicago, where she campaigned against the use of chemicals in food to mask poor quality. Field's first husband, John Dean Caton, commissioned this portrait on the occasion of their honeymoon in Paris.

JULY
S	M	T	W	T	F	S
		1	2	3	4	5
6	7	8	9	10	11	12
13	14	15	16	17	18	19
20	21	22	23	24	25	26
27	28	29	30	31		

AUGUST
S	M	T	W	T	F	S
					1	2
3	4	5	6	7	8	9
10	11	12	13	14	15	16
17	18	19	20	21	22	23
24	25	26	27	28	29	30
31						

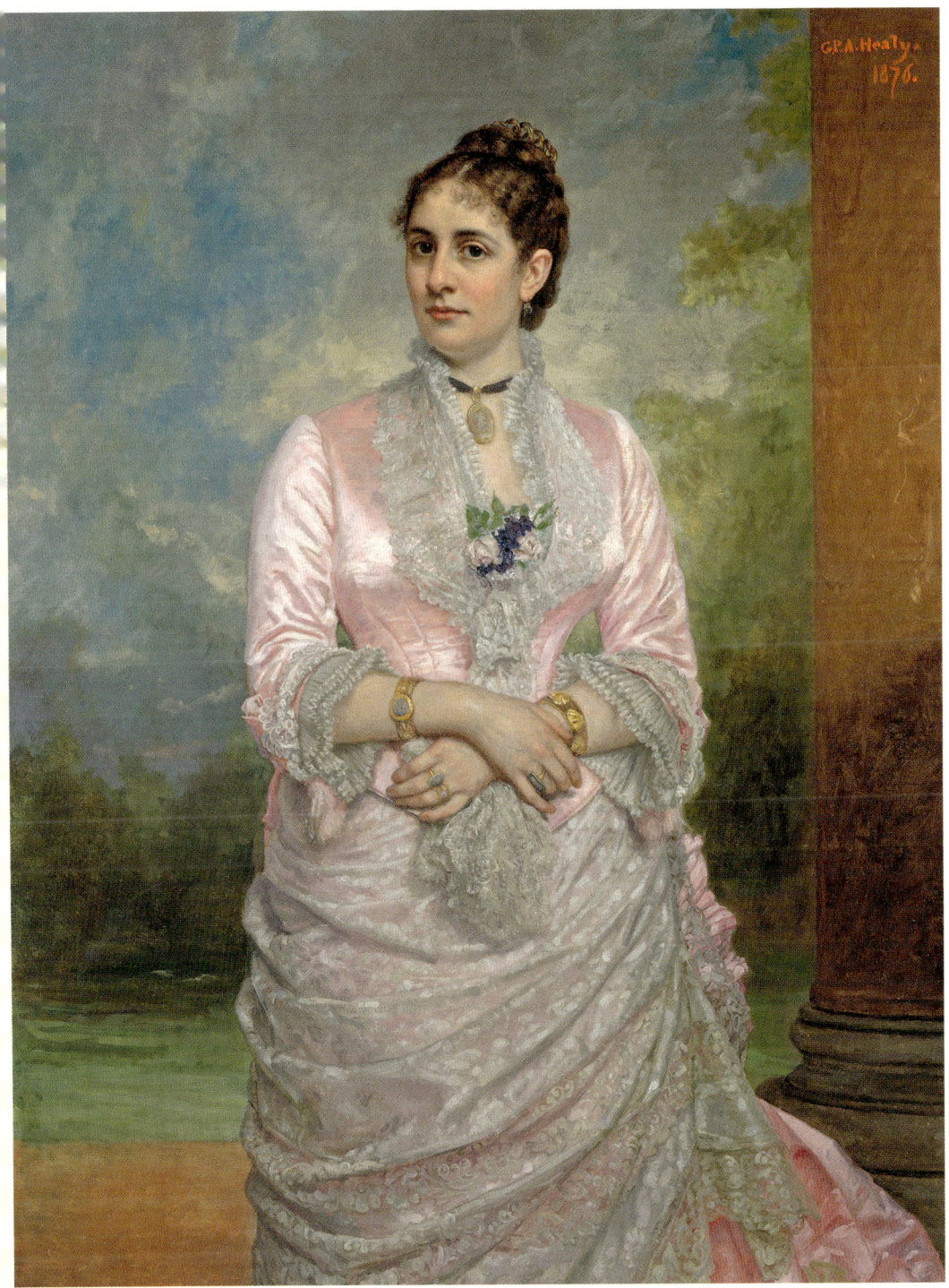

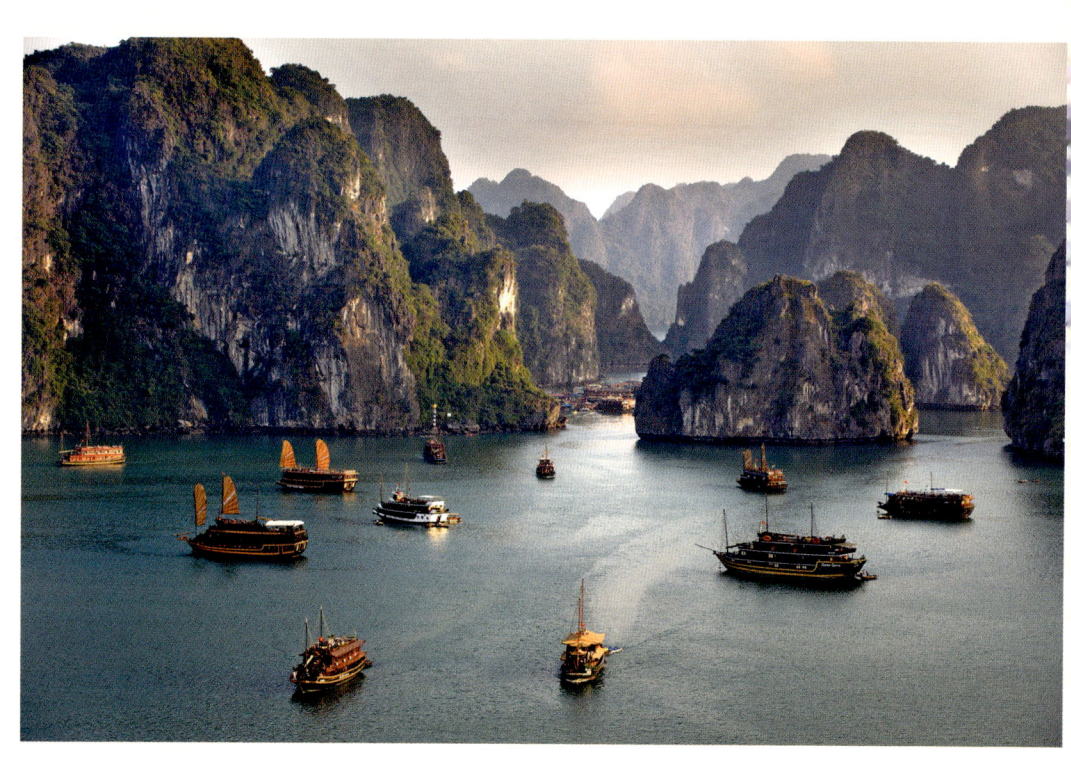

Traditional Vietnamese junks amid the limestone islands of Ha Long Bay
Digital photo
by Reed Kaestner
Corbis, Getty Images
Ha Long, Vietnam
Smithsonian Journeys

Ha Long Bay is a spectacular seascape sculpted by nature, with more than 1,600 limestone karst islands rising from emerald-green waters as pillars and various other shapes. Praised in poetry and painting, Ha Long Bay has been recognized as a UNESCO World Heritage Site for its outstanding beauty and geological value.

JULY

S	M	T	W	T	F	S
		1	2	3	4	5
6	7	8	9	10	11	12
13	14	15	16	17	18	19
20	21	22	23	24	25	26
27	28	29	30	31		

AUGUST

S	M	T	W	T	F	S
					1	2
3	4	5	6	7	8	9
10	11	12	13	14	15	16
17	18	19	20	21	22	23
24	25	26	27	28	29	30
31						

JULY

SUNDAY
13

MONDAY
14

TUESDAY
15

WEDNESDAY
16

THURSDAY
17

FRIDAY
18

SATURDAY
19

JULY

SUNDAY
20

MONDAY
21

TUESDAY
22

WEDNESDAY
23

THURSDAY ●
24

FRIDAY
25
MUHARRAM ENDS (SUNDOWN)

SATURDAY
26

Teri Greeves (Kiowa, b. 1970) and Dennis Esquivel (Grand Traverse Band of Ottawa and Chippewa, b. 1970)
Ah-Day: The Favorite One's Chair, 2022
Santa Fe, NM
Cherry wood, glass beads, deer hide, metal, and brass tacks
38 × 13 × 19 in.
(96.5 × 33 × 48.3 cm)
Cooper Hewitt, Smithsonian Design Museum

Artists Teri Greeves and Dennis Esquivel created this child's chair to honor the birth of their first child and "all Kiowa ah-days, past and present." "Ah-day" refers to a child's place as the favored member of a Kiowa family. The chair's form was inspired by Kiowa cradleboards and bags worn by Kiowa women. The deer-hide seat and back feature colorful glass beadwork by Greeves, echoing traditional abstract designs.

JULY
S	M	T	W	T	F	S
		1	2	3	4	5
6	7	8	9	10	11	12
13	14	15	16	17	18	19
20	21	22	23	24	25	26
27	28	29	30	31		

AUGUST
S	M	T	W	T	F	S
					1	2
3	4	5	6	7	8	9
10	11	12	13	14	15	16
17	18	19	20	21	22	23
24	25	26	27	28	29	30
31						

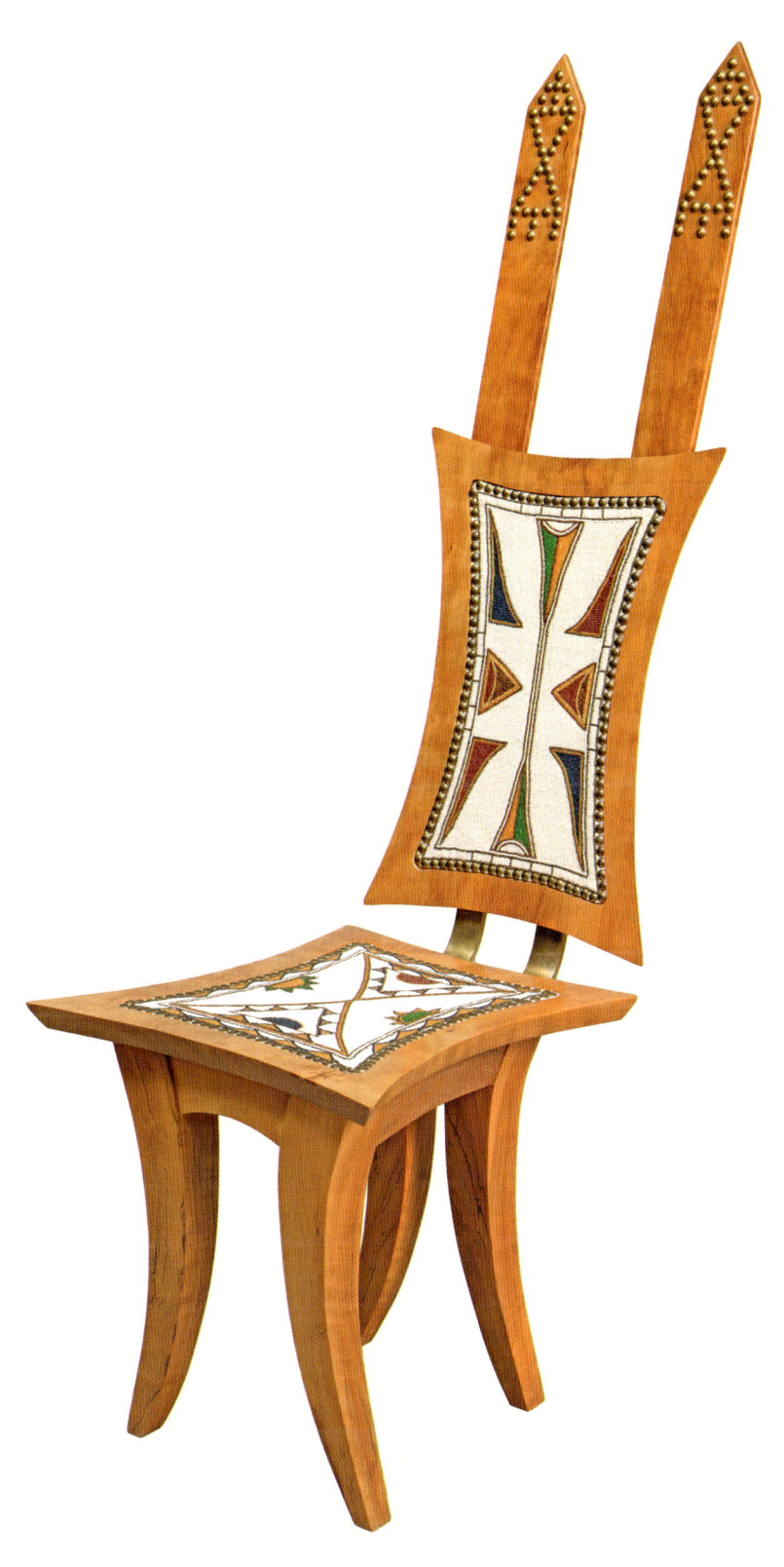

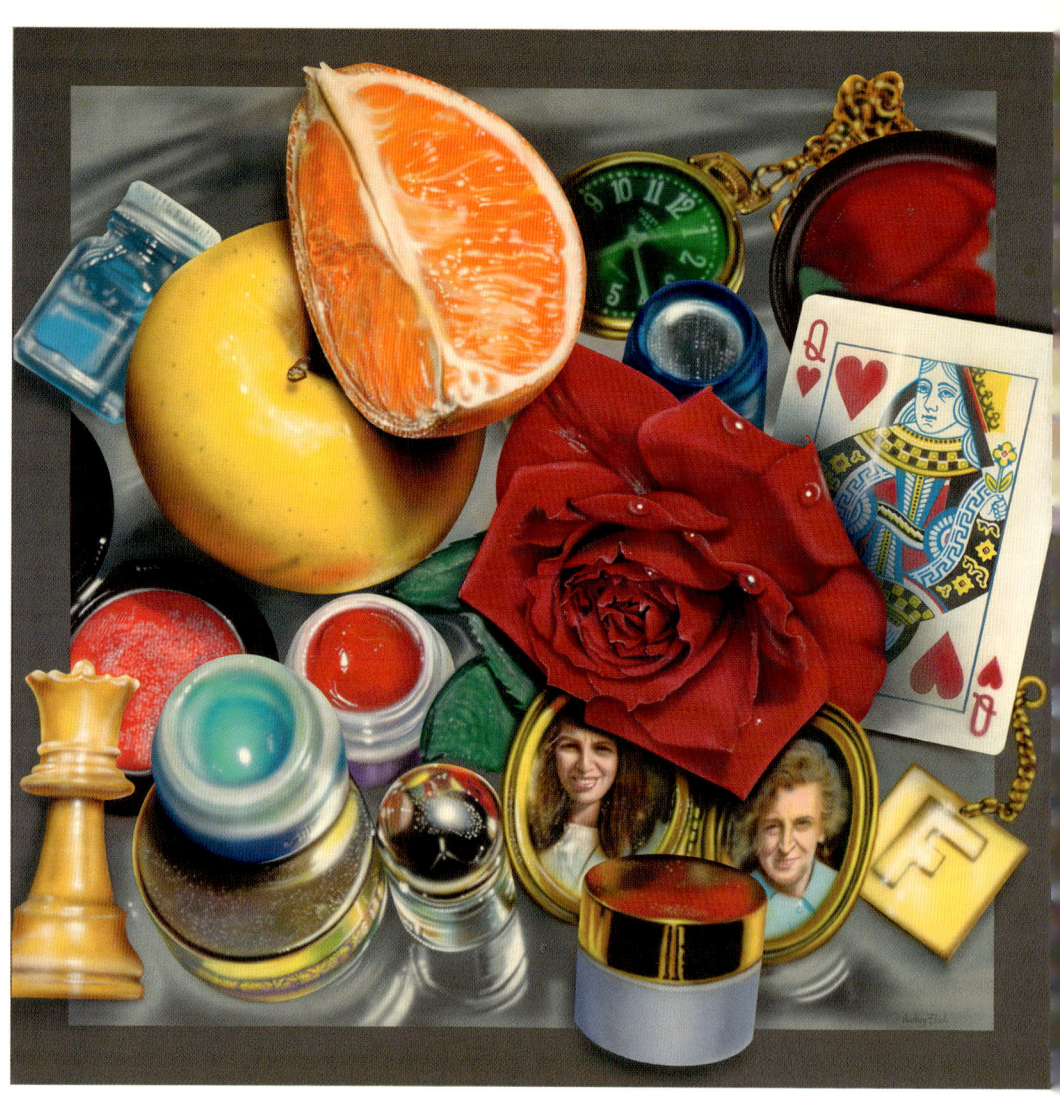

JULY · AUGUST

Audrey Flack (b. 1931)
Queen, 1976
Acrylic on canvas
80 × 80 in. (203 × 203 cm)
Gift of Louis K.
and Susan P. Meisel
Smithsonian American
Art Museum

Audrey Flack's *Queen* is full of symbols, including a pocket watch, a dewy rose, and a juicy slice of orange. Flack has said that she made the painting "for all women, particularly women gamblers"—a specific reference to her mother, whose portrait appears in the open locket just below the queen of hearts playing card. Flack also depicted another queen here: the most powerful piece in the game of chess and an emblem of female power and importance.

JULY
S	M	T	W	T	F	S
		1	2	3	4	5
6	7	8	9	10	11	12
13	14	15	16	17	18	19
20	21	22	23	24	25	26
27	28	29	30	31		

AUGUST
S	M	T	W	T	F	S
					1	2
3	4	5	6	7	8	9
10	11	12	13	14	15	16
17	18	19	20	21	22	23
24	25	26	27	28	29	30
31						

SUNDAY
27

MONDAY
28

TUESDAY
29

WEDNESDAY
30

THURSDAY
31

FRIDAY
1

SATURDAY
2

AUGUST

SUNDAY
3

MONDAY
4

TUESDAY
5

WEDNESDAY
6

THURSDAY
7

FRIDAY
8

SATURDAY ○
9

DJ Kool Herc with sound system at T-Connection, 1980
Polaroid
4⅛ × 3¼ in. (10.5 × 8.3 cm)
National Museum of African American History and Culture

In the early 1970s Jamaican American Clive Campbell, aka DJ Kool Herc (b. 1955), experimented with playing records at parties in New York, laying a foundation for what would become hip-hop. This Polaroid print shows DJ Kool Herc in 1980 at the T-Connection club in the Bronx, NY, with elements of the sound system he used during the 1970s and early 1980s.

AUGUST
S	M	T	W	T	F	S
					1	2
3	4	5	6	7	8	9
10	11	12	13	14	15	16
17	18	19	20	21	22	23
24	25	26	27	28	29	30
31						

SEPTEMBER
S	M	T	W	T	F	S
	1	2	3	4	5	6
7	8	9	10	11	12	13
14	15	16	17	18	19	20
21	22	23	24	25	26	27
28	29	30				

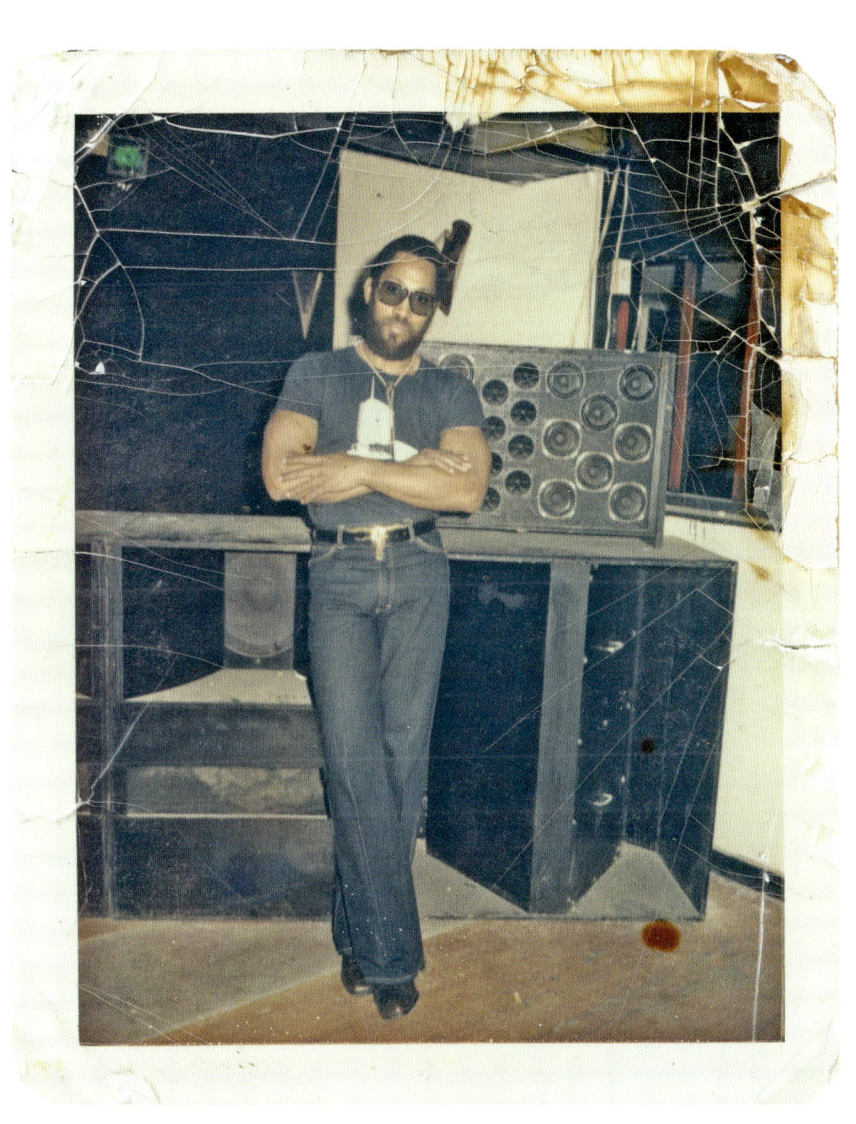

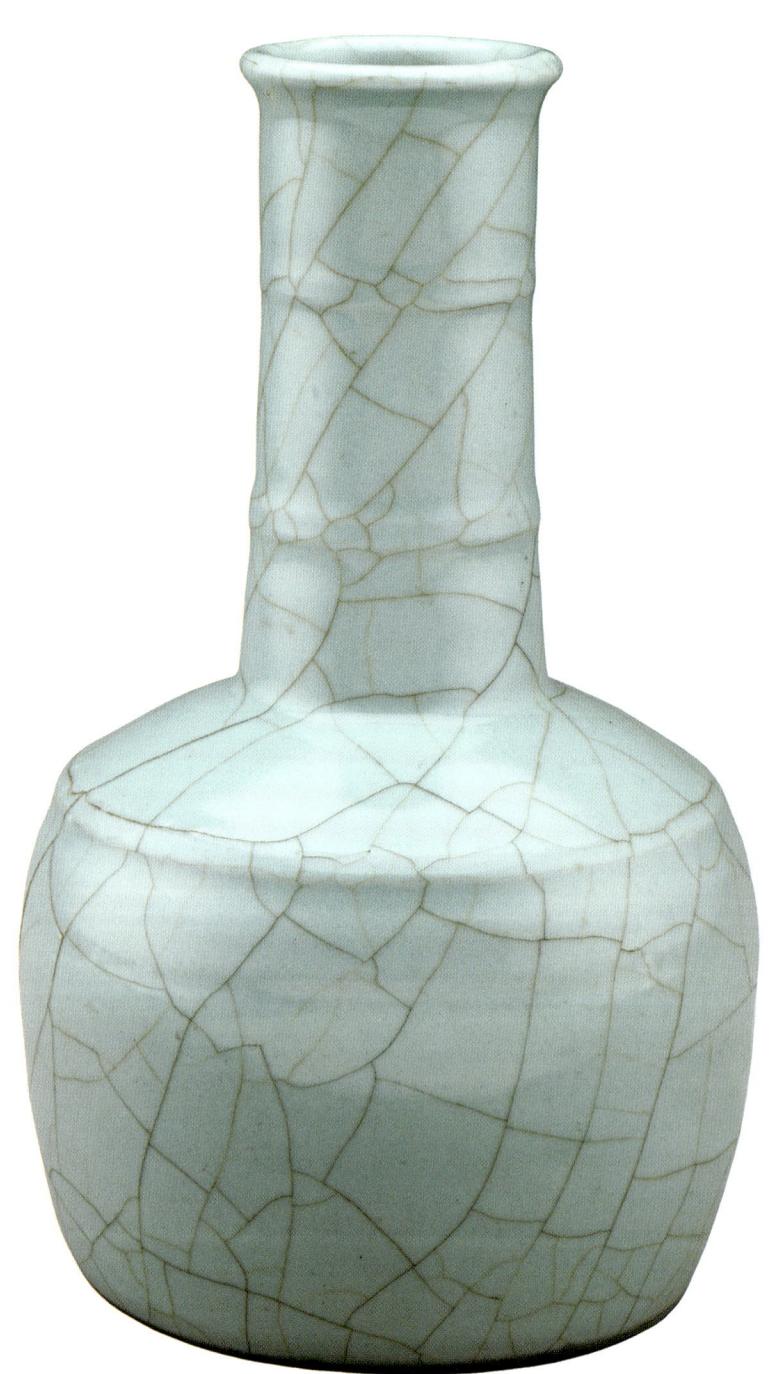

AUGUST

Long-necked vessel with raised-bow-string decoration, 12th century Southern Song dynasty, China
Guan ware: stoneware with glaze
9⅛ × 5 9/16 in. (23.2 × 14.1 cm)
Gift of Charles Lang Freer
National Museum of Asian Art

This Guan-ware bottle, perhaps a vase, was fired at the imperial kilns of the Southern Song dynasty (1127–1279). Distinguished by a dark clay body and thick bluish-gray-green glaze, Guan wares display an intentionally induced subtle pattern reminiscent of cracked ice. The bottle accords with the dynasty's aesthetic of elegant simplicity. To create the crackle pattern, potters applied a low-silica glaze in multiple layers and controlled the cooling process of the kiln to encourage different rates of expansion and contraction of the body and the glaze.

AUGUST
S	M	T	W	T	F	S
					1	2
3	4	5	6	7	8	9
10	11	12	13	14	15	16
17	18	19	20	21	22	23
24	25	26	27	28	29	30
31						

SEPTEMBER
S	M	T	W	T	F	S
	1	2	3	4	5	6
7	8	9	10	11	12	13
14	15	16	17	18	19	20
21	22	23	24	25	26	27
28	29	30				

SUNDAY
10

MONDAY
11

TUESDAY
12

WEDNESDAY
13

THURSDAY
14

FRIDAY
15

SATURDAY
16

AUGUST

SUNDAY
17

MONDAY
18

TUESDAY
19

WEDNESDAY
20

THURSDAY
21

FRIDAY
22

SATURDAY
23

Adebisi Fabunmi
(b. 1945, Takoradi, Ghana)
City in the Moon, 1960s
Woodcut on paper
24¼ × 19⅛ in.
(61.6 × 48.6 cm)
Bequest of Bernice M. Kelly
National Museum
of African Art

Adebisi Fabunmi, also known as FAB, has long been interested in cities, particularly his adopted hometown of Oshogbo, Nigeria. In an era when news of US missions to the moon dominated the global imagination, Fabunmi offered a Nigerian-centered vision of what a future lunar urban landscape might look like—or, perhaps, what astronauts might discover upon arrival.

AUGUST
S	M	T	W	T	F	S
					1	2
3	4	5	6	7	8	9
10	11	12	13	14	15	16
17	18	19	20	21	22	23
24	25	26	27	28	29	30
31						

SEPTEMBER
S	M	T	W	T	F	S
	1	2	3	4	5	6
7	8	9	10	11	12	13
14	15	16	17	18	19	20
21	22	23	24	25	26	27
28	29	30				

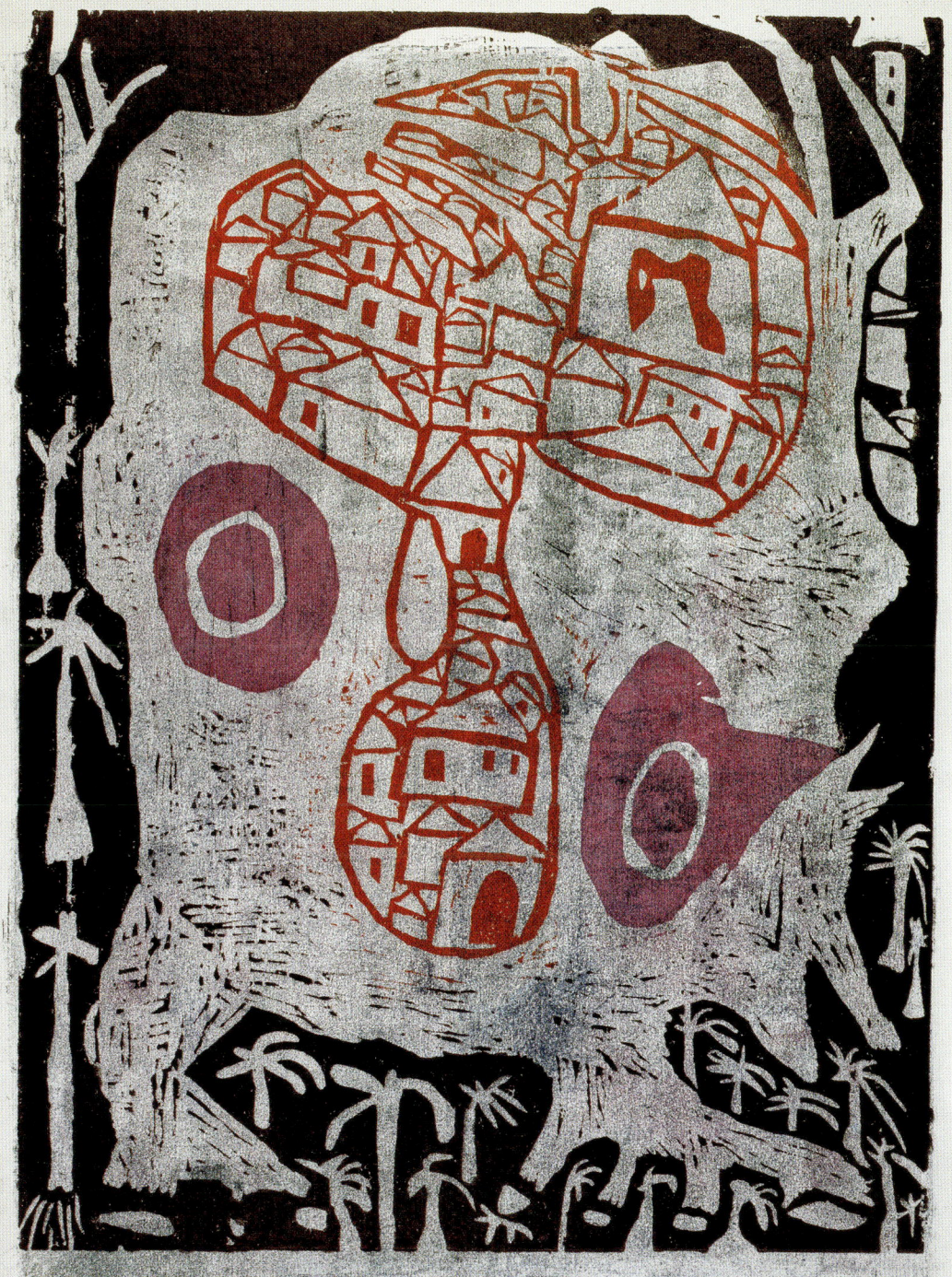

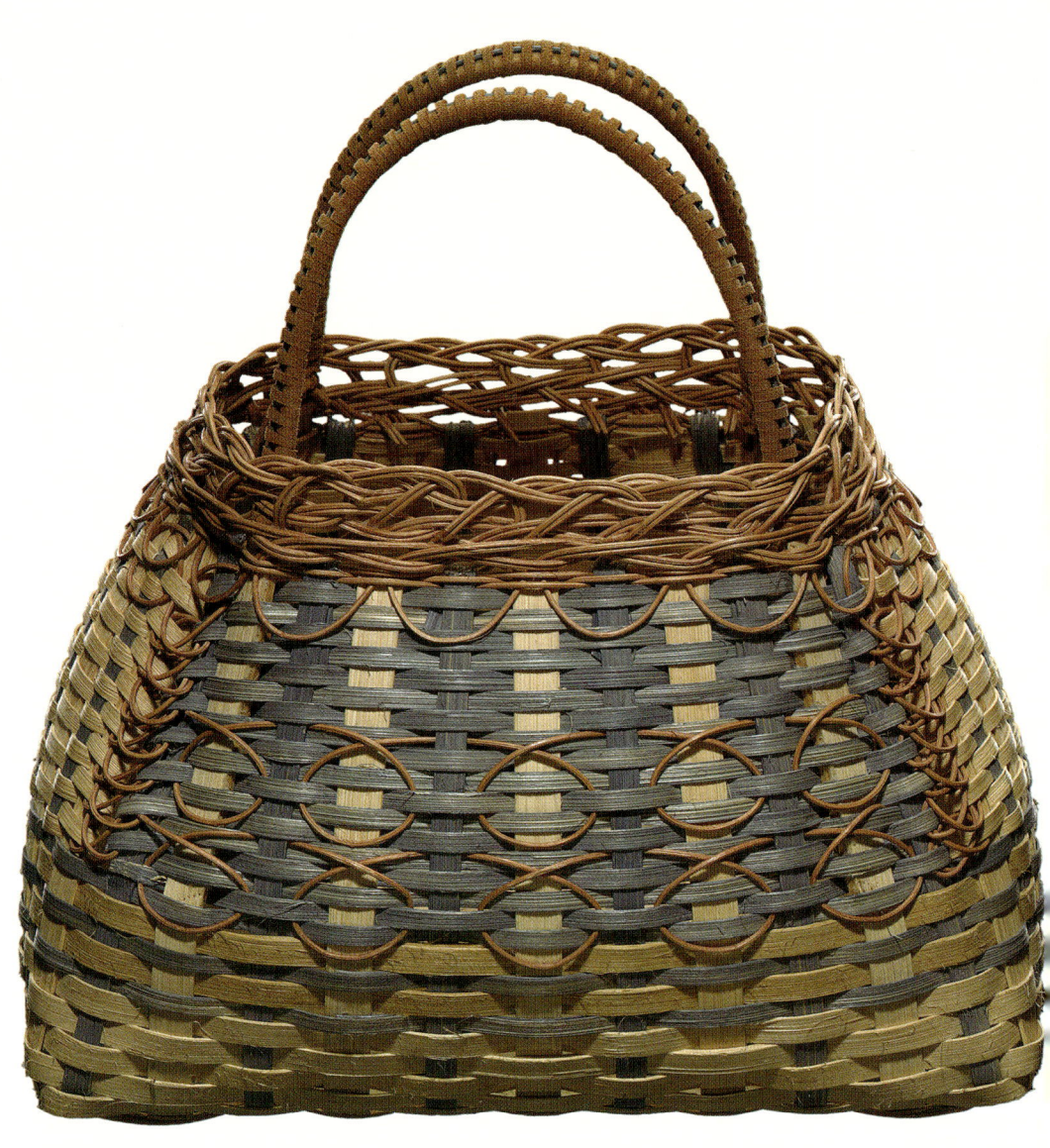

Rodslen Brown
(Black/Cherokee Nation
of Oklahoma, 1960–2020)
Lace Moxie's Purse, 2014
Muskogee, OK
Root runners, flat reed,
dye, hide
14 × 14 × 10 in.
(36 × 36 × 25 cm)
National Museum
of the American Indian

The intricate weaving in this basket expresses the idea that, whether by blood or kinship, Freemen and Native Americans are intertwined and the histories of Freedmen and Black Native Americans are part of Native history. The placement of each runner and reed speaks to the care and attention that goes into observing, learning, and translating culture.
It is part of the *Ancestors Know Who We Are* online exhibition, which ignites a conversation on the experiences of Black Indigenous women through art.

AUGUST

SUNDAY
24

MONDAY
25

TUESDAY
26

WEDNESDAY
27

THURSDAY
28

FRIDAY
29

SATURDAY
30

AUGUST
S	M	T	W	T	F	S
					1	2
3	4	5	6	7	8	9
10	11	12	13	14	15	16
17	18	19	20	21	22	23
24	25	26	27	28	29	30
31						

SEPTEMBER
S	M	T	W	T	F	S
	1	2	3	4	5	6
7	8	9	10	11	12	13
14	15	16	17	18	19	20
21	22	23	24	25	26	27
28	29	30				

AUGUST · SEPTEMBER

SUNDAY
31
☾

MONDAY — LABOR DAY (US AND CAN.)
1

TUESDAY
2

WEDNESDAY
3

THURSDAY
4

FRIDAY
5

SATURDAY
6

Messier 43, a part of the Orion star-forming complex, in near-infrared light
Artistic processing by Yuri Beletsky, Carnegie Observatories; data acquisition/reduction by Igor Chilingarian and Brian McLeod, October 30–31, 2012
Magellan Clay 6.5-m Telescope
Las Campanas Observatory, Chile
Smithsonian Astrophysical Observatory

This image depicts the northern outskirts of the Great Orion Nebula, about half of the Lunar disk across, in near-infrared light at the wavelength between 1 and 2.2 microns invisible to a human's eye. The brightest object in the image, NU Ori, is a hot and massive young star whose winds blew a bubble around it. Bright red filaments are made of warm molecular hydrogen.

AUGUST
S	M	T	W	T	F	S
					1	2
3	4	5	6	7	8	9
10	11	12	13	14	15	16
17	18	19	20	21	22	23
24	25	26	27	28	29	30
31						

SEPTEMBER
S	M	T	W	T	F	S
	1	2	3	4	5	6
7	8	9	10	11	12	13
14	15	16	17	18	19	20
21	22	23	24	25	26	27
28	29	30				

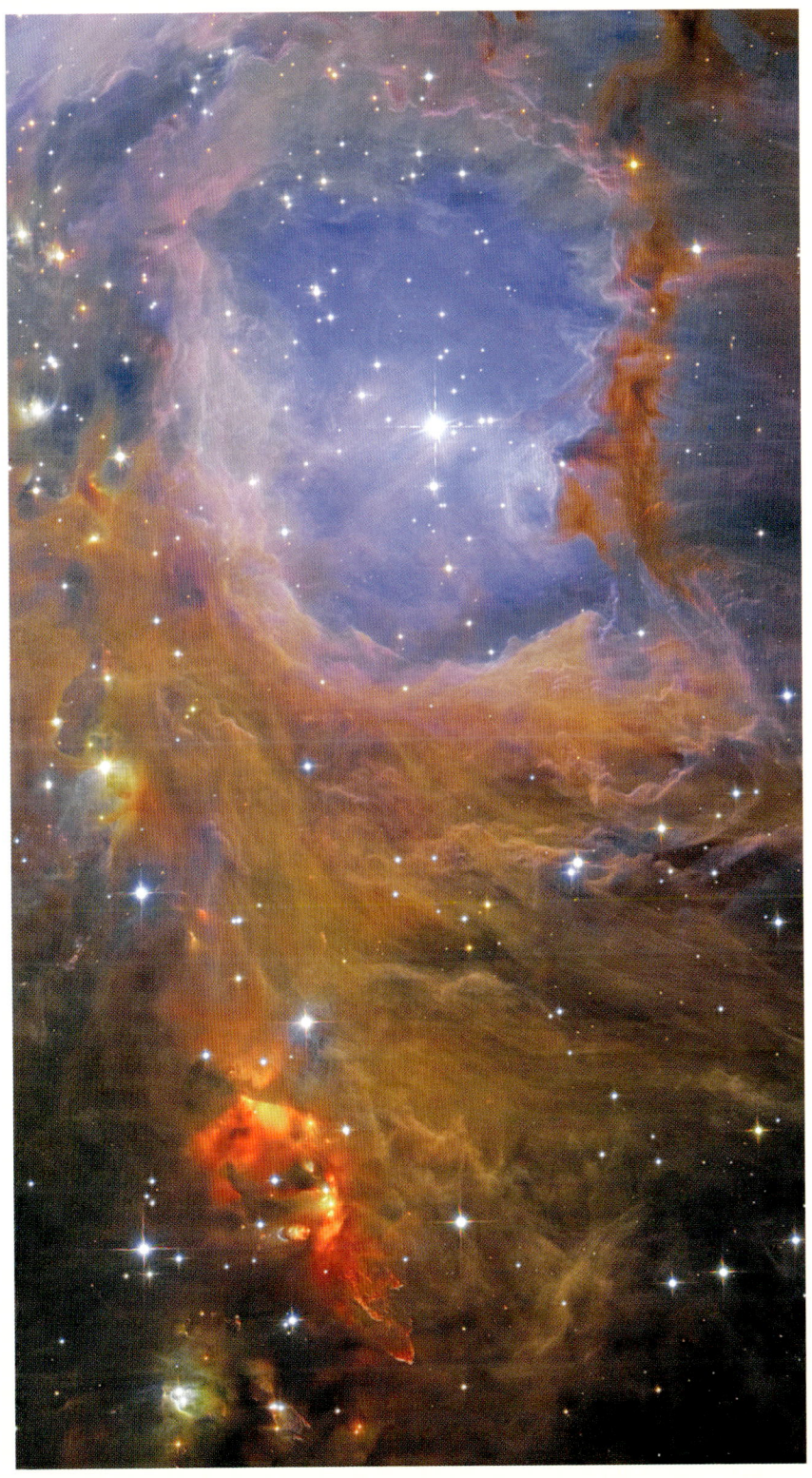

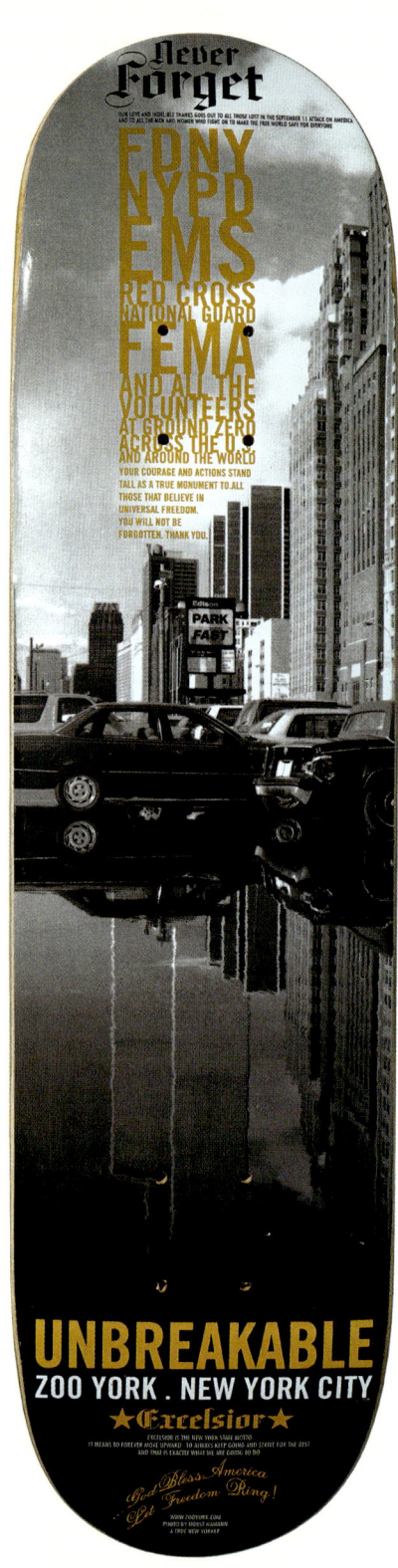

SEPTEMBER

Limited Edition 9/11 Tribute Skate Deck, 2001
Designed by Eli Morgan Gesner (b. 1970)
Zoo York, New York, NY
Wood, ink
31 × 7½ × 2 in. (78.7 × 19.1 × 5.1 cm)
National Museum of American History

This skateboard deck by Zoo York commemorates the 9/11 first responders. Designer Eli Morgan Gesner used photographer Horst Hamann's image of the New York City skyline, replacing the fallen towers with a tribute to 9/11 first responders but leaving the standing towers reflected in the water at the bottom. This deck is from the original limited run of 100.

SEPTEMBER

S	M	T	W	T	F	S
	1	2	3	4	5	6
7	8	9	10	11	12	13
14	15	16	17	18	19	20
21	22	23	24	25	26	27
28	29	30				

OCTOBER

S	M	T	W	T	F	S
			1	2	3	4
5	6	7	8	9	10	11
12	13	14	15	16	17	18
19	20	21	22	23	24	25
26	27	28	29	30	31	

SUNDAY
7

MONDAY
8

TUESDAY
9

WEDNESDAY
10

THURSDAY
11

FRIDAY
12

SATURDAY
13

SEPTEMBER

SUNDAY
14

MONDAY
15

TUESDAY
16

WEDNESDAY
17

THURSDAY
18

FRIDAY
19

SATURDAY
20

Lesley Vance (b. 1977)
Untitled, 2021
Oil on linen
31 × 24 in. (78.7 × 61 cm)
Gift of Iris
and Adam Singer
Hirshhorn Museum and
Sculpture Garden

Lesley Vance creates sweeping abstract paintings with a palpable sense of flow and surfaces that weave light and shadow, color and form, background and foreground. This heady mix almost appears to vibrate before the eyes like an optical illusion.

SEPTEMBER

S	M	T	W	T	F	S
	1	2	3	4	5	6
7	8	9	10	11	12	13
14	15	16	17	18	19	20
21	22	23	24	25	26	27
28	29	30				

OCTOBER

S	M	T	W	T	F	S
			1	2	3	4
5	6	7	8	9	10	11
12	13	14	15	16	17	18
19	20	21	22	23	24	25
26	27	28	29	30	31	

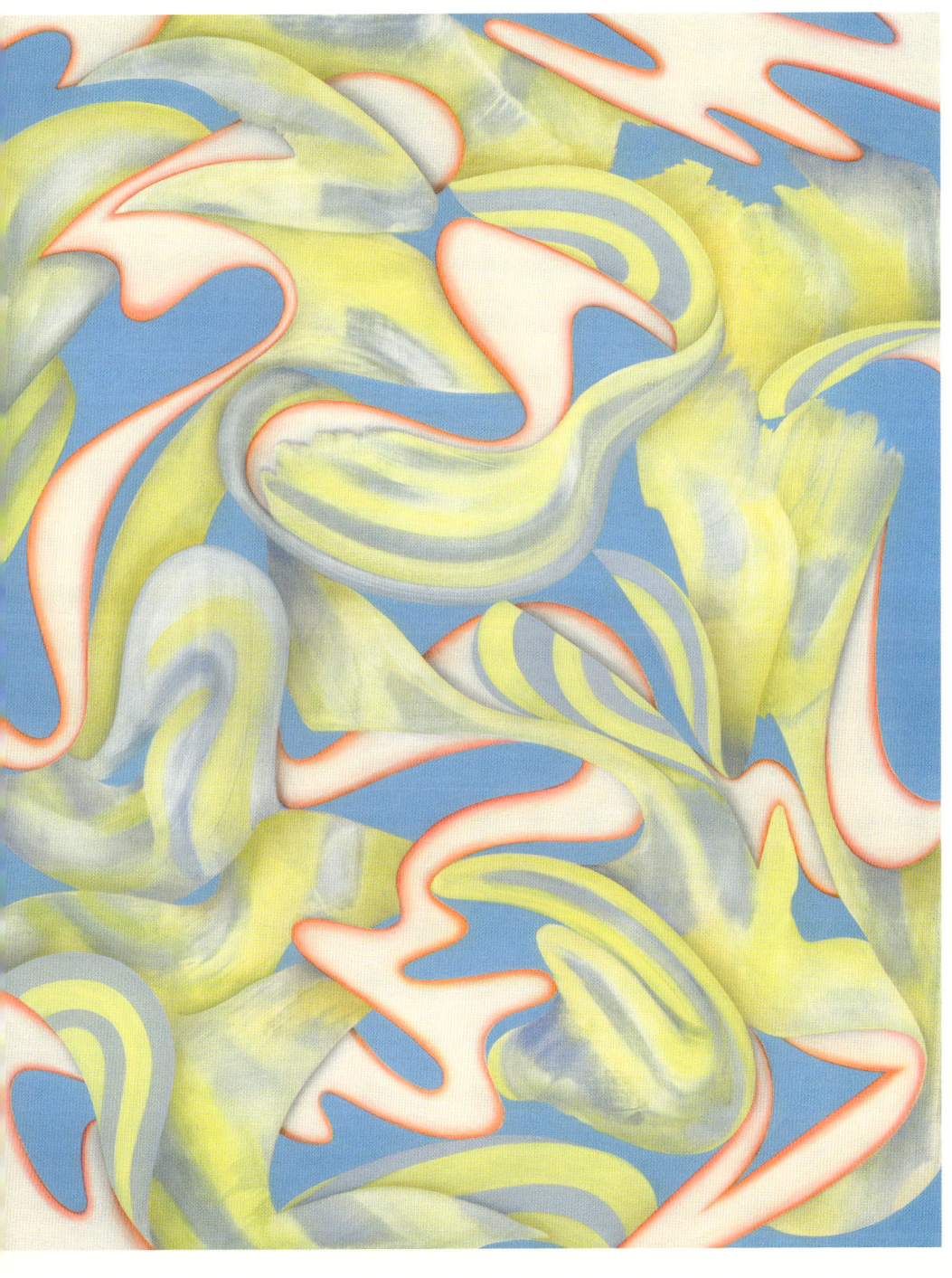

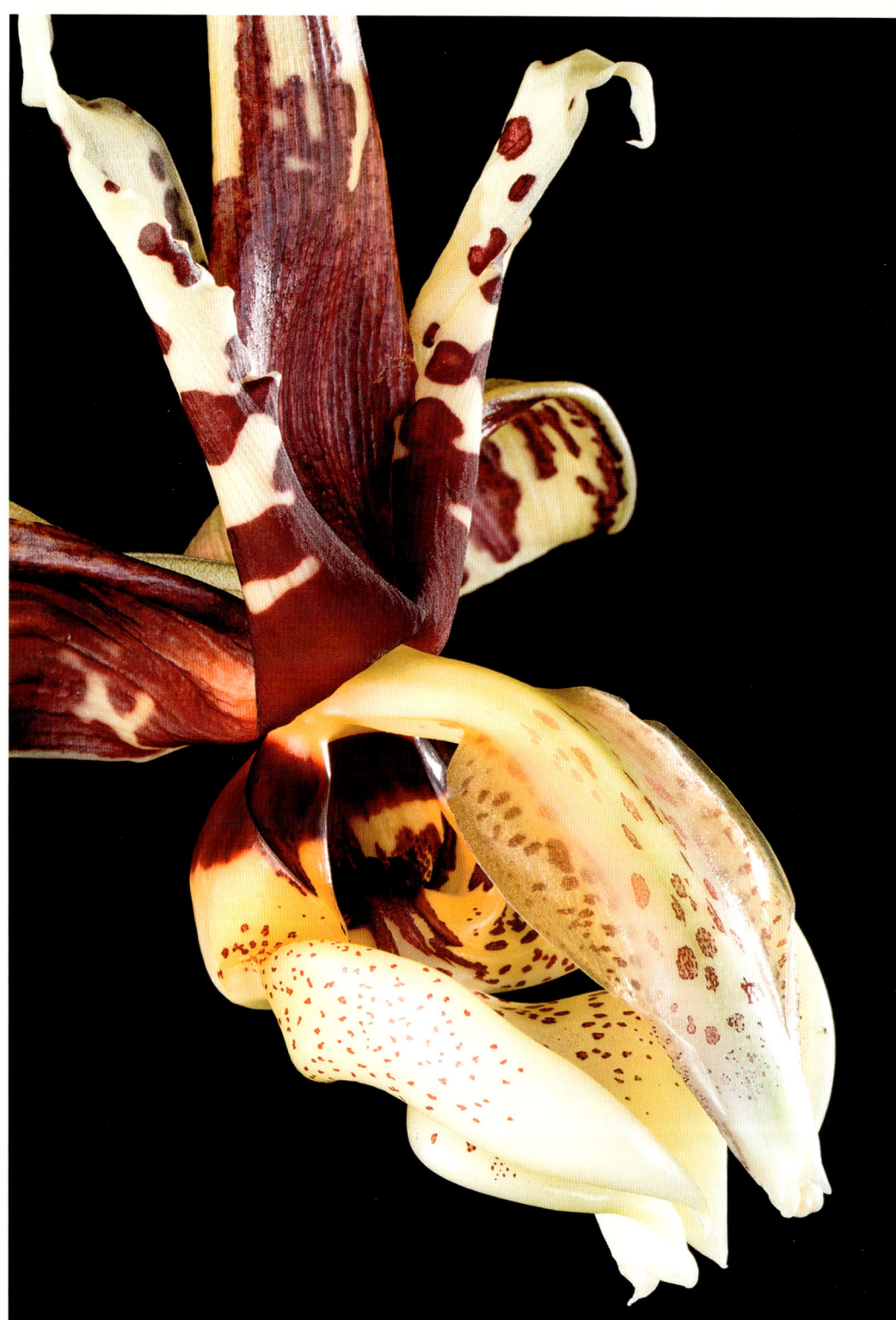

SEPTEMBER

Tiger-like Stanhopea (*Stanhopea tigrina*) orchid
Digital image by Hannele Lahti, June 2023
Washington, DC
Smithsonian Gardens

Stanhopea tigrina, an orchid native to the rainforests of Mexico, features clusters of heavily spotted flowers that can reach up to eight inches in diameter. Its sweet scent attracts male *Euglossine* bees that collect fragrance compounds from the flower's "lips" to use in their courtship displays.

SUNDAY 21 ●

MONDAY 22
FIRST DAY OF AUTUMN
ROSH HASHANAH BEGINS (SUNDOWN)

TUESDAY 23

WEDNESDAY 24
ROSH HASHANAH ENDS (SUNDOWN)

THURSDAY 25

FRIDAY 26

SATURDAY 27

SEPTEMBER
S	M	T	W	T	F	S
	1	2	3	4	5	6
7	8	9	10	11	12	13
14	15	16	17	18	19	20
21	22	23	24	25	26	27
28	29	30				

OCTOBER
S	M	T	W	T	F	S
			1	2	3	4
5	6	7	8	9	10	11
12	13	14	15	16	17	18
19	20	21	22	23	24	25
26	27	28	29	30	31	

SEPTEMBER · OCTOBER

SUNDAY
28

MONDAY ☽
29

TUESDAY
30

WEDNESDAY   YOM KIPPUR BEGINS (SUNDOWN)
1

THURSDAY   YOM KIPPUR ENDS (SUNDOWN)
2

FRIDAY
3

SATURDAY
4

Kepler technology demonstration camera, 2000
Created by the National Aeronautics and Space Administration
Invar, super-invar, brass tubes, steel components, wiring, electronics, and duct tape
2 ft. 5 in. × 2 ft. 5 in. × 7 ft. 7 in., 863 lb. (74 × 74 × 231 cm, 391.5 kg)
National Air and Space Museum

This testbed simulation proved that a proposed charge-coupled device (CCD) photometer, which measures the brightness of a star in an image, could detect the incredibly small changes in light caused when an Earth-size exoplanet crosses between its star and the Earth. The successful experiment encouraged NASA to develop the Kepler Space Telescope mission, which discovered thousands of planets orbiting other stars.

SEPTEMBER

S	M	T	W	T	F	S
	1	2	3	4	5	6
7	8	9	10	11	12	13
14	15	16	17	18	19	20
21	22	23	24	25	26	27
28	29	30				

OCTOBER

S	M	T	W	T	F	S
			1	2	3	4
5	6	7	8	9	10	11
12	13	14	15	16	17	18
19	20	21	22	23	24	25
26	27	28	29	30	31	

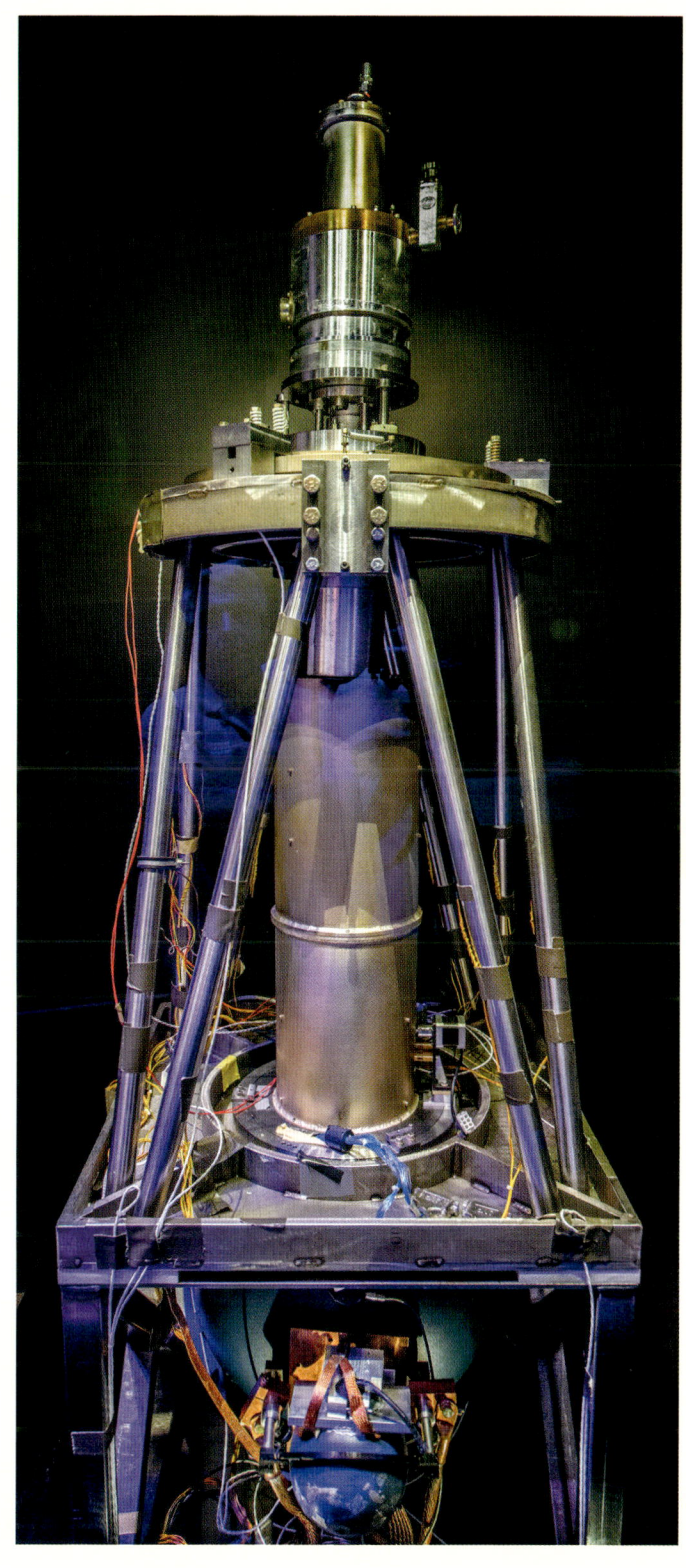

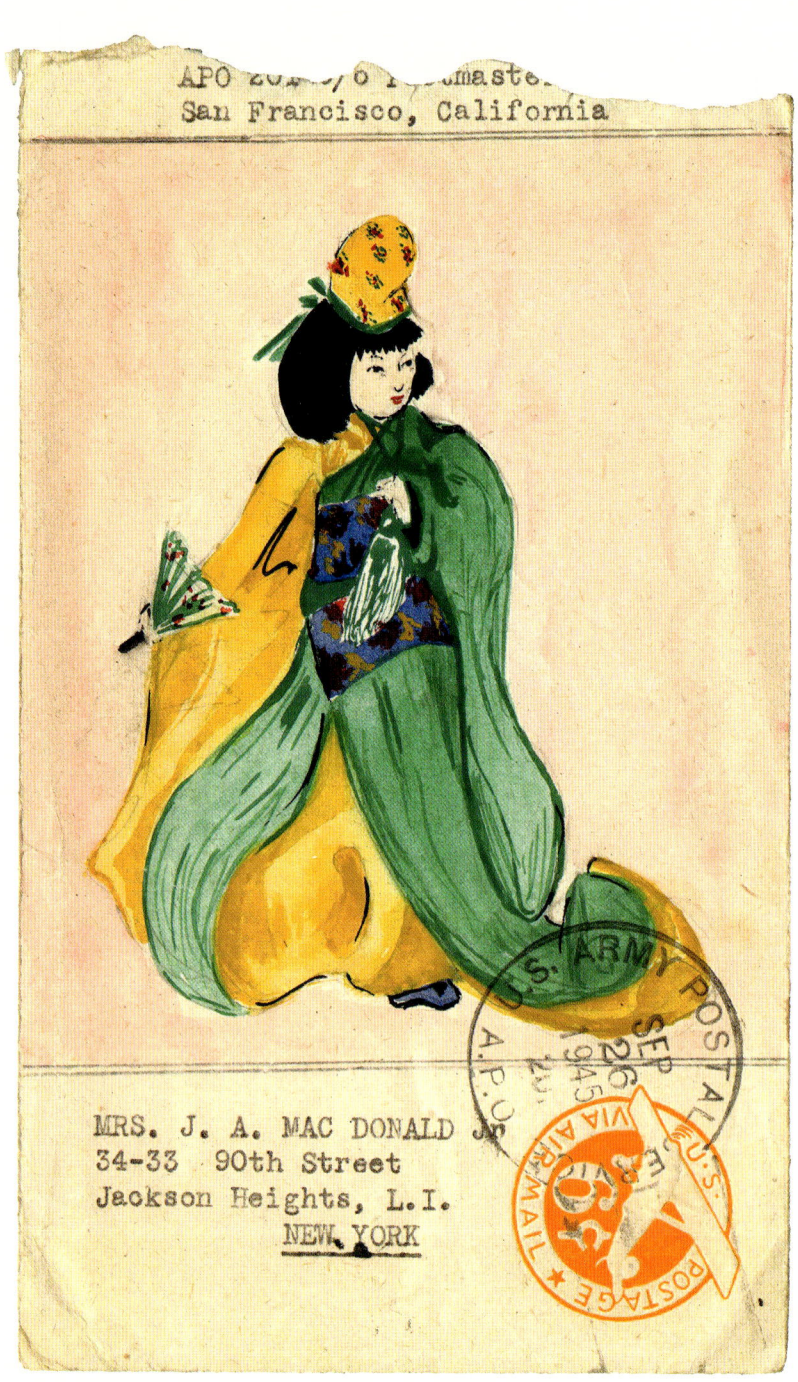

Jack Fogarty (1920–2016)
Hand-illustrated airmail envelope, 1945
Paper, ink, watercolor
3¾ × 6⁵⁄₁₆ in. (9.5 × 16 cm)
National Postal Museum

This postal stationery airmail envelope sent from Yokohama, Japan, to New York was passed by a censor (#31527) and postmarked September 26, 1945. The watercolor by Jack Fogarty depicts a female figure in Japanese dress, which he refers to in the enclosed letter to Mary MacDonald. Sgt. Fogarty sent this correspondence a few weeks after his unit, the 98th Evacuation Hospital, treated Prime Minister Hideki Tojo for self-inflected gunshot wounds resulting from his September 8 suicide attempt made in reaction to Japan's surrender to the United States.

OCTOBER

S	M	T	W	T	F	S
			1	2	3	4
5	6	7	8	9	10	11
12	13	14	15	16	17	18
19	20	21	22	23	24	25
26	27	28	29	30	31	

NOVEMBER

S	M	T	W	T	F	S
						1
2	3	4	5	6	7	8
9	10	11	12	13	14	15
16	17	18	19	20	21	22
23	24	25	26	27	28	29
30						

OCTOBER

SUNDAY
5

MONDAY
6

TUESDAY
7

WEDNESDAY
8

THURSDAY
9

FRIDAY
10

SATURDAY
11

OCTOBER

SUNDAY
12

MONDAY COLUMBUS DAY / INDIGENOUS PEOPLES' DAY (US) ☽
THANKSGIVING DAY (CAN.)
13

TUESDAY
14

WEDNESDAY
15

THURSDAY
16

FRIDAY
17

SATURDAY
18

Meagon Anishinabie
(Oji-Cree Treaty 5, b. 1992)
Earrings, 2022
Birch bark, moose hide, beadwork
11 × 6 × ¼ in.
(28 × 15 × .6 cm)
Smithsonian Institution Traveling Exhibition Service

Knowing Nature: Stories of the Boreal Forest / Historias del bosque boreal focuses on the biodiversity and global importance of our northernmost forests through first-person stories, authentic objects such as these earrings, interactive experiences, and exquisite photography and videography. The exhibition integrates the themes of climate change, Indigenous perspectives, and the relationship between people and nature, offering stories of resilience, strength, and hope in a changing world.

OCTOBER
S	M	T	W	T	F	S
			1	2	3	4
5	6	7	8	9	10	11
12	13	14	15	16	17	18
19	20	21	22	23	24	25
26	27	28	29	30	31	

NOVEMBER
S	M	T	W	T	F	S
						1
2	3	4	5	6	7	8
9	10	11	12	13	14	15
16	17	18	19	20	21	22
23	24	25	26	27	28	29
30						

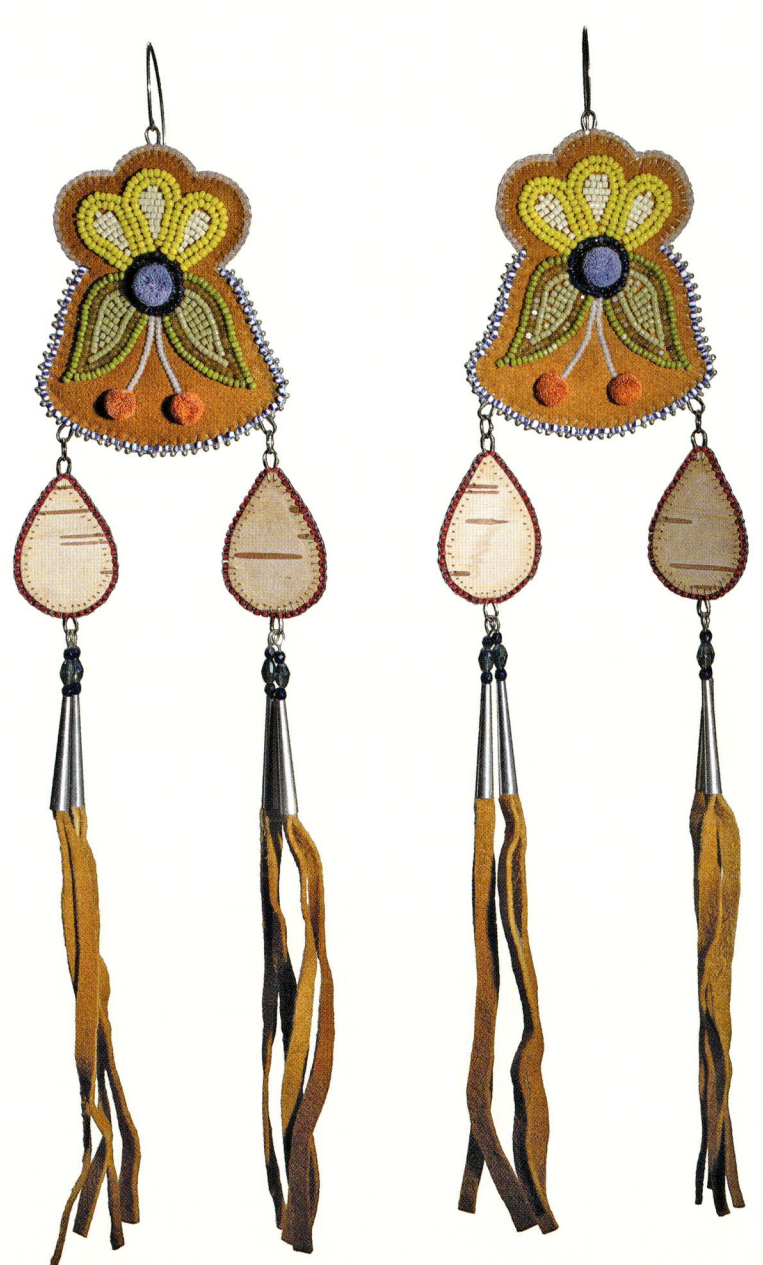

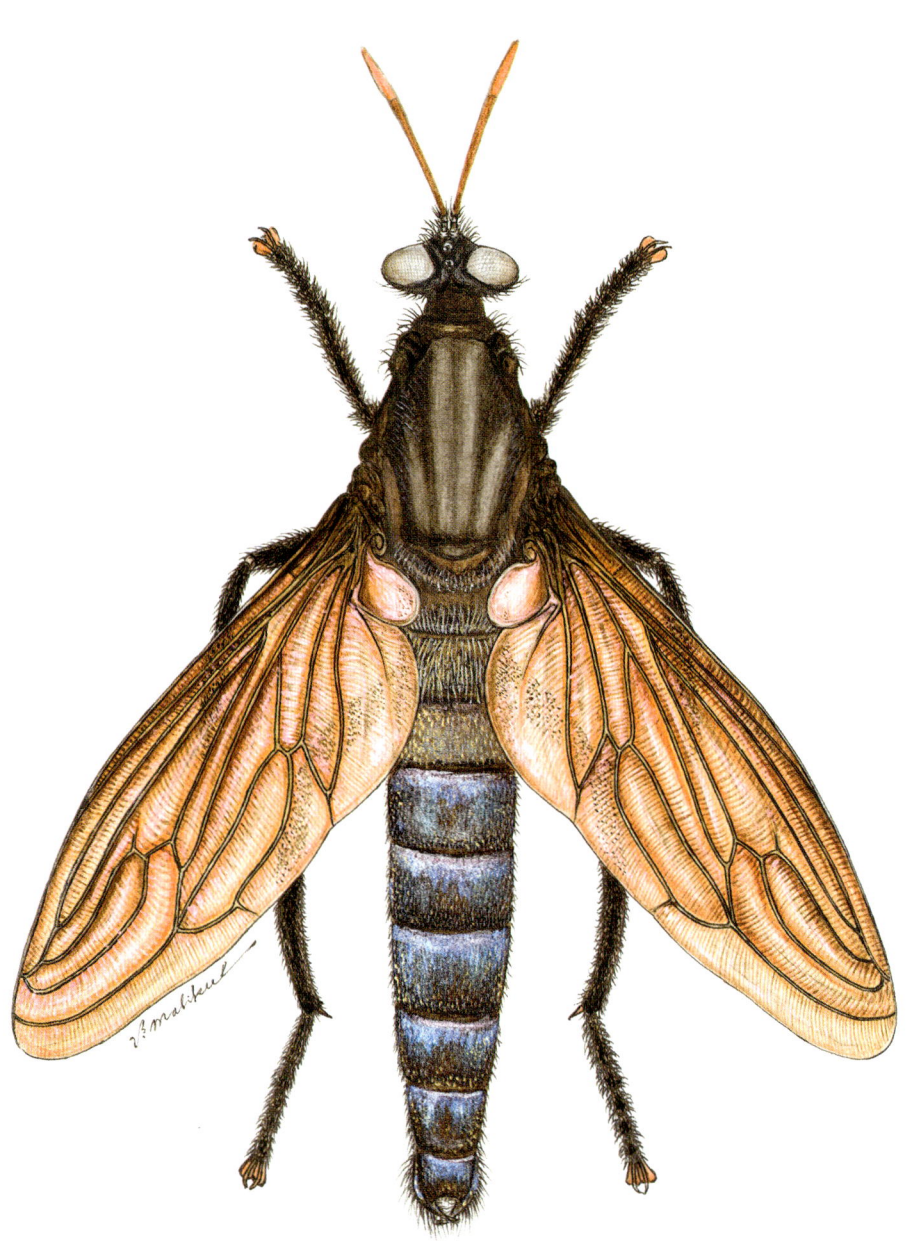

Vichai Malikul (b. 1942)
Illustration of
Gauromydas heros Perty, 1833
Iridescent acrylic
watercolor on paper
9 × 12 in. (22.8 × 30.5 cm)
National Museum
of Natural History

This illustration of the giant fly *Gauromydas heros* is based on a specimen in the Smithsonian's entomology collections. Scientific illustrator Vichai Malikul used iridescent inks to replicate the shifting, luminous, metallic colors of the species' body. With a body length of nearly three inches and a wingspan of four inches, *Gauromydas heros* is the largest known species of fly.

OCTOBER

S	M	T	W	T	F	S
			1	2	3	4
5	6	7	8	9	10	11
12	13	14	15	16	17	18
19	20	21	22	23	24	25
26	27	28	29	30	31	

NOVEMBER

S	M	T	W	T	F	S
						1
2	3	4	5	6	7	8
9	10	11	12	13	14	15
16	17	18	19	20	21	22
23	24	25	26	27	28	29
30						

OCTOBER

SUNDAY
19

DIWALI

MONDAY
20

TUESDAY
21

WEDNESDAY
22

THURSDAY
23

FRIDAY
24

SATURDAY
25

OCTOBER · NOVEMBER

SUNDAY
26

MONDAY
27

TUESDAY
28

WEDNESDAY
29

THURSDAY
30

FRIDAY   HALLOWEEN
31

SATURDAY
1

Walter Schnackenberg (1880–1961)
Der Salamander, 1920
From *Schnackenberg: Kostüme, Plakate und Dekorationen*, 1920
Lithograph on paper
10.2 × 13.4 in. (26 × 34 cm)
Gift of James Howard Fraser
Smithsonian Libraries and Archives

Artist Walter Schnackenberg studied art in Germany and worked as a painter, illustrator, poster artist, and set and costume designer for the theater. The book *Schnackenberg: Kostüme, Plakate und Dekorationen* aptly represents the diversity of his work and is held in the collections of the Cooper Hewitt, Smithsonian Design Library.

OCTOBER

S	M	T	W	T	F	S
			1	2	3	4
5	6	7	8	9	10	11
12	13	14	15	16	17	18
19	20	21	22	23	24	25
26	27	28	29	30	31	

NOVEMBER

S	M	T	W	T	F	S
						1
2	3	4	5	6	7	8
9	10	11	12	13	14	15
16	17	18	19	20	21	22
23	24	25	26	27	28	29
30						

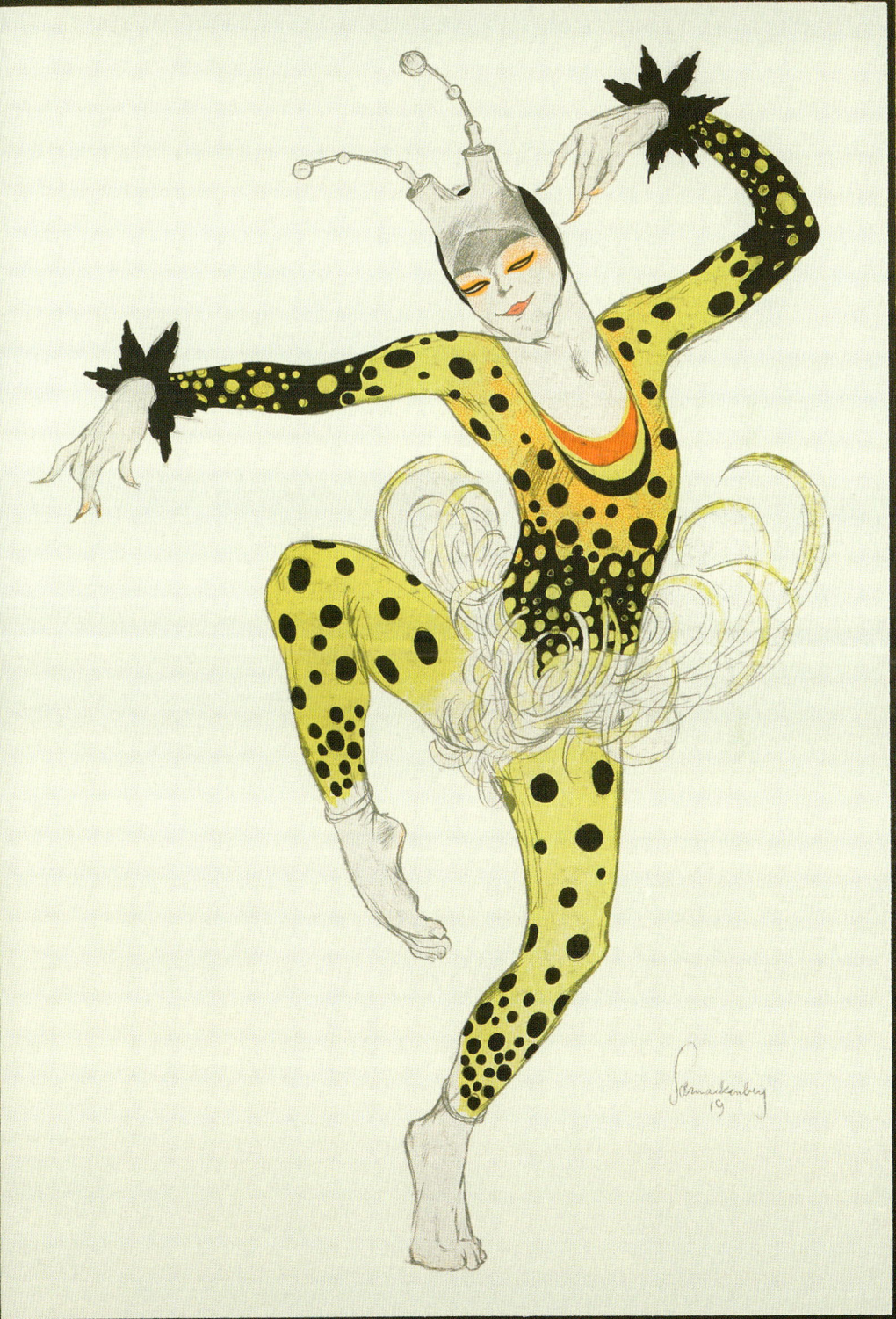

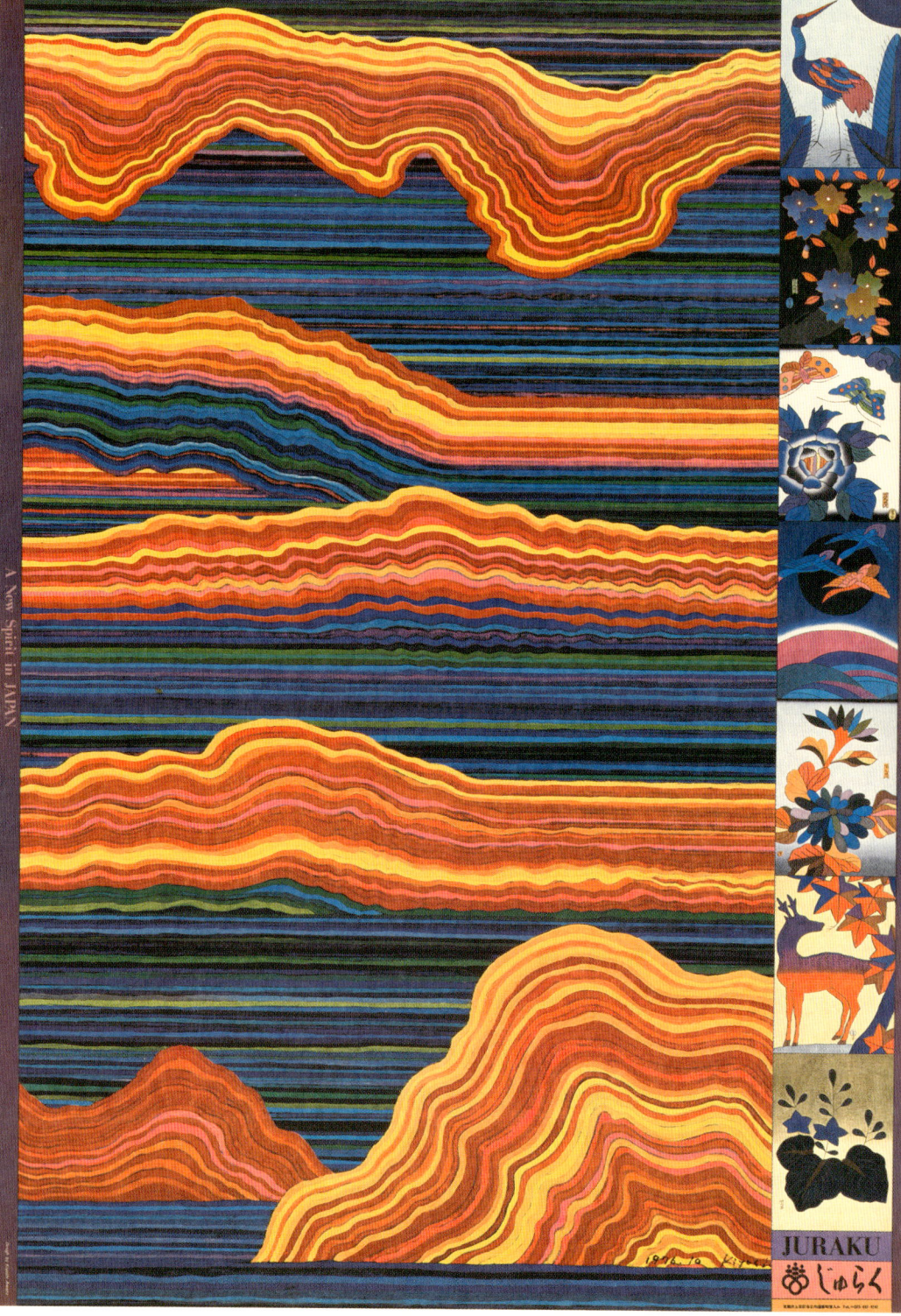

NOVEMBER

Poster for *A New Spirit in Japan*, c. 1984
Designed by Kiyoshi Awazu (1929–2009), for the kimono company Juraku Japan
Lithograph on paper
40 11/16 × 28 11/16 in. (103.3 × 72.8 cm)
Gift of James Howard Fraser
Cooper Hewitt, Smithsonian Design Museum

Kiyoshi Awazu was well known for his experimental approach to graphic design, and he often drew upon his previous art pieces, a production method he called "graphism." The image on the left is a painting he created in 1976, and the illustrations on the right edge are selected works from his woodblock prints series produced in 1981.

NOVEMBER						
S	M	T	W	T	F	S
						1
2	3	4	5	6	7	8
9	10	11	12	13	14	15
16	17	18	19	20	21	22
23	24	25	26	27	28	29
30						

DECEMBER						
S	M	T	W	T	F	S
	1	2	3	4	5	6
7	8	9	10	11	12	13
14	15	16	17	18	19	20
21	22	23	24	25	26	27
28	29	30	31			

DAYLIGHT SAVING TIME ENDS

SUNDAY
2

MONDAY
3

ELECTION DAY (US)

TUESDAY
4

○ WEDNESDAY
5

THURSDAY
6

FRIDAY
7

SATURDAY
8

NOVEMBER

SUNDAY
9

MONDAY
10

TUESDAY · VETERANS DAY (US) · REMEMBRANCE DAY (CAN.)
11

WEDNESDAY
12

THURSDAY
13

FRIDAY
14

SATURDAY
15

Volunteer firefighter badge, 1861
Charleston, SC
Engraved silver
1¼ × ¾ in. (3.2 × 1.9 cm)
National Museum of American History

During and after the Civil War, Black firefighters in Charleston established their own volunteer companies. Formerly municipal auxiliaries under white officers, these men organized units like Niagara Fire Company No. 8. They elected officers, gained incorporation from the state, and petitioned for formal recognition by the Charleston Fire Department.

NOVEMBER

S	M	T	W	T	F	S
						1
2	3	4	5	6	7	8
9	10	11	12	13	14	15
16	17	18	19	20	21	22
23	24	25	26	27	28	29
30						

DECEMBER

S	M	T	W	T	F	S
	1	2	3	4	5	6
7	8	9	10	11	12	13
14	15	16	17	18	19	20
21	22	23	24	25	26	27
28	29	30	31			

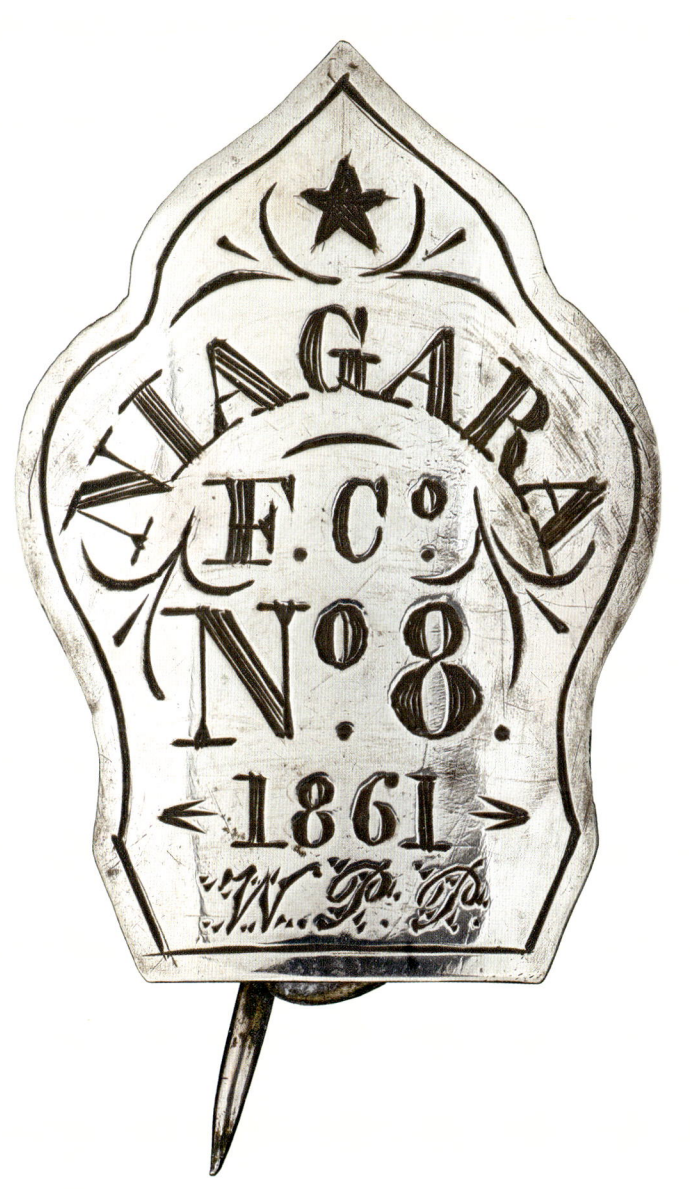

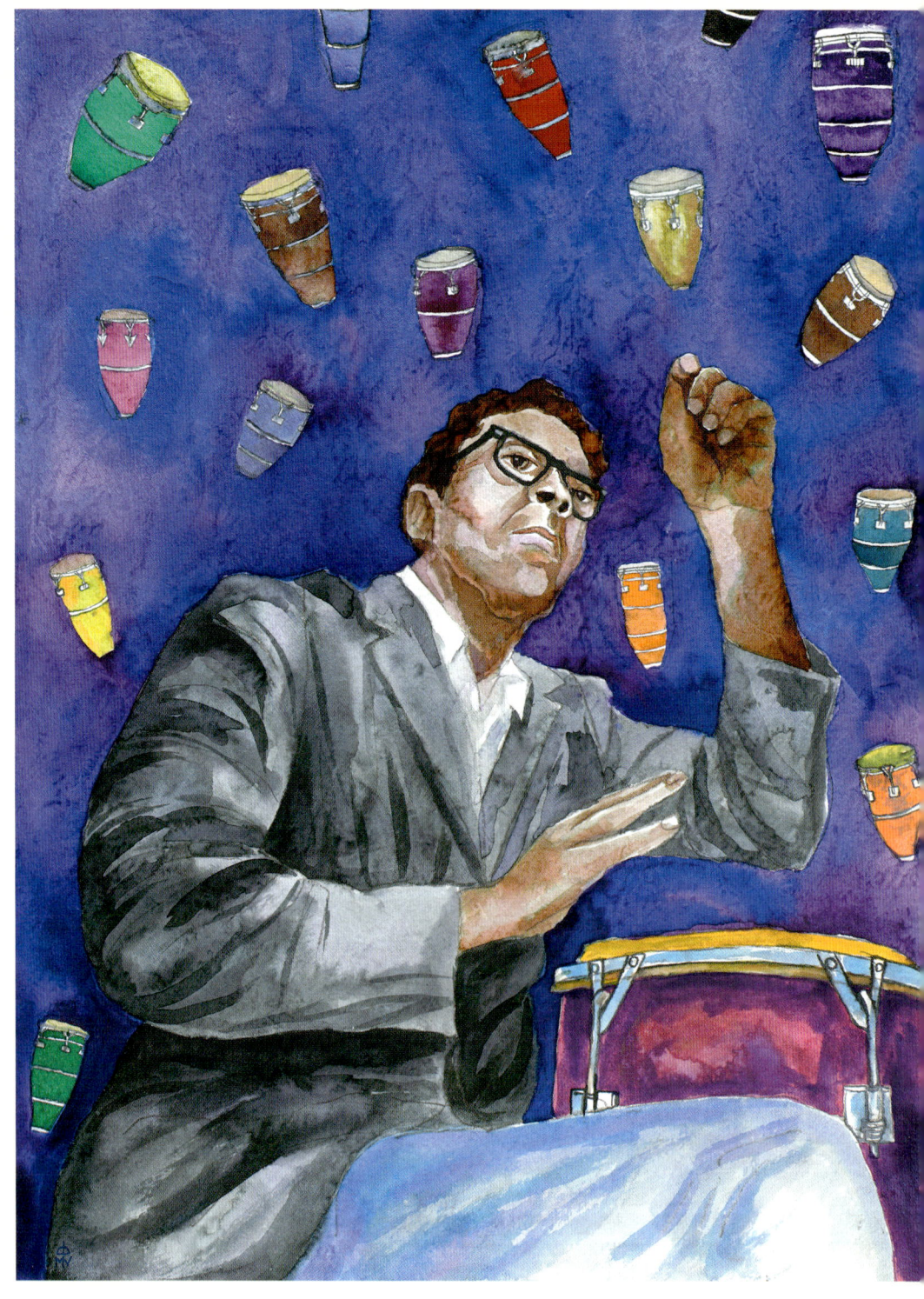

Manny Vega (b. 1956)
Ray Barretto, 2021
Watercolor on Arches paper
30¾ × 22³⁄₁₆ in.
(78.1 × 56.4 cm)
National Portrait Gallery

This portrait depicts the towering percussionist and bandleader Ray Barretto (1929–2006), whose five-decade career starting in the late 1950s showcased the vital exchanges between jazz and salsa. The artist Manny Vega painted the "King of Hard Hands" immersed in a solo and set against a deep purple background with miniature congas floating in space.

NOVEMBER

S	M	T	W	T	F	S
						1
2	3	4	5	6	7	8
9	10	11	12	13	14	15
16	17	18	19	20	21	22
23	24	25	26	27	28	29
30						

DECEMBER

S	M	T	W	T	F	S
	1	2	3	4	5	6
7	8	9	10	11	12	13
14	15	16	17	18	19	20
21	22	23	24	25	26	27
28	29	30	31			

NOVEMBER

SUNDAY
16

MONDAY
17

TUESDAY
18

WEDNESDAY
19

THURSDAY
20

FRIDAY
21

SATURDAY
22

NOVEMBER

SUNDAY
23

MONDAY
24

TUESDAY
25

WEDNESDAY
26

THURSDAY
27
THANKSGIVING DAY (US)

FRIDAY
28
◐

SATURDAY
29

Donation tin for the
Mary McLeod Bethune
Memorial Fund, early 1960s
National Council of
Negro Women
Washington, DC
Paint, tin
4⁹⁄₁₆ × 3³⁄₈ × 1⁹⁄₁₆ in.
(11.6 × 8.5 × 4 cm)
National Museum of
African American History
and Culture

Mary McLeod Bethune
(1875–1955) was an
educator, activist, philan-
thropist, and founder
of the National Council of
Negro Women. In the early
1960s members of this
organization used this
donation tin to raise funds
to erect a memorial to
Bethune. In 1974 their
vision was realized when
a statue of Bethune was
unveiled in Lincoln Park
in Washington, DC.

NOVEMBER

S	M	T	W	T	F	S
						1
2	3	4	5	6	7	8
9	10	11	12	13	14	15
16	17	18	19	20	21	22
23	24	25	26	27	28	29
30						

DECEMBER

S	M	T	W	T	F	S
	1	2	3	4	5	6
7	8	9	10	11	12	13
14	15	16	17	18	19	20
21	22	23	24	25	26	27
28	29	30	31			

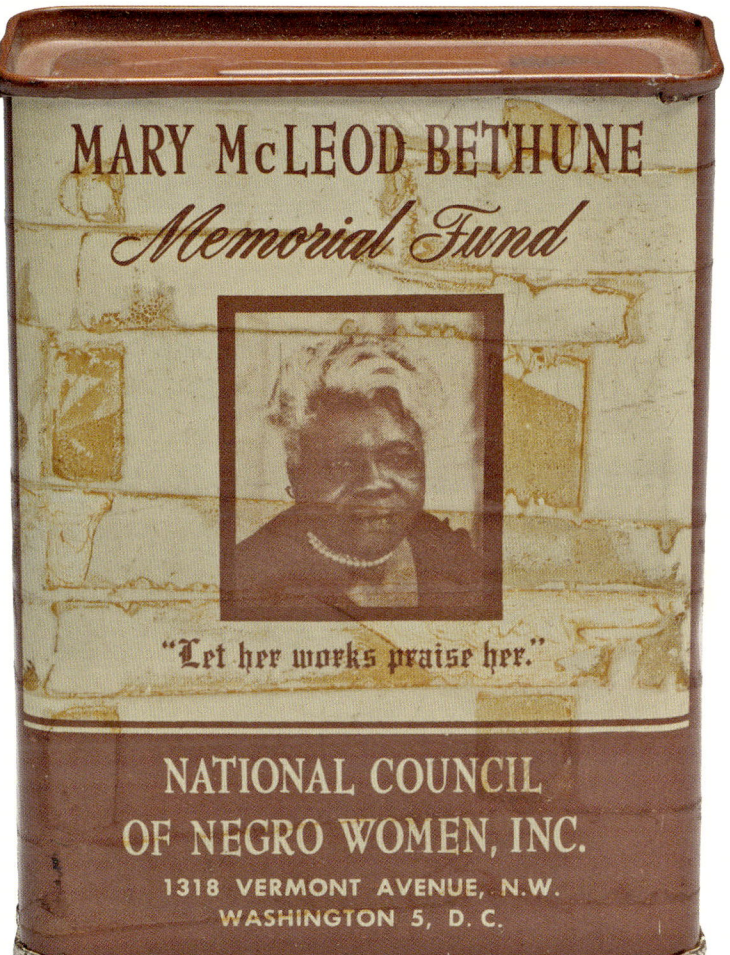

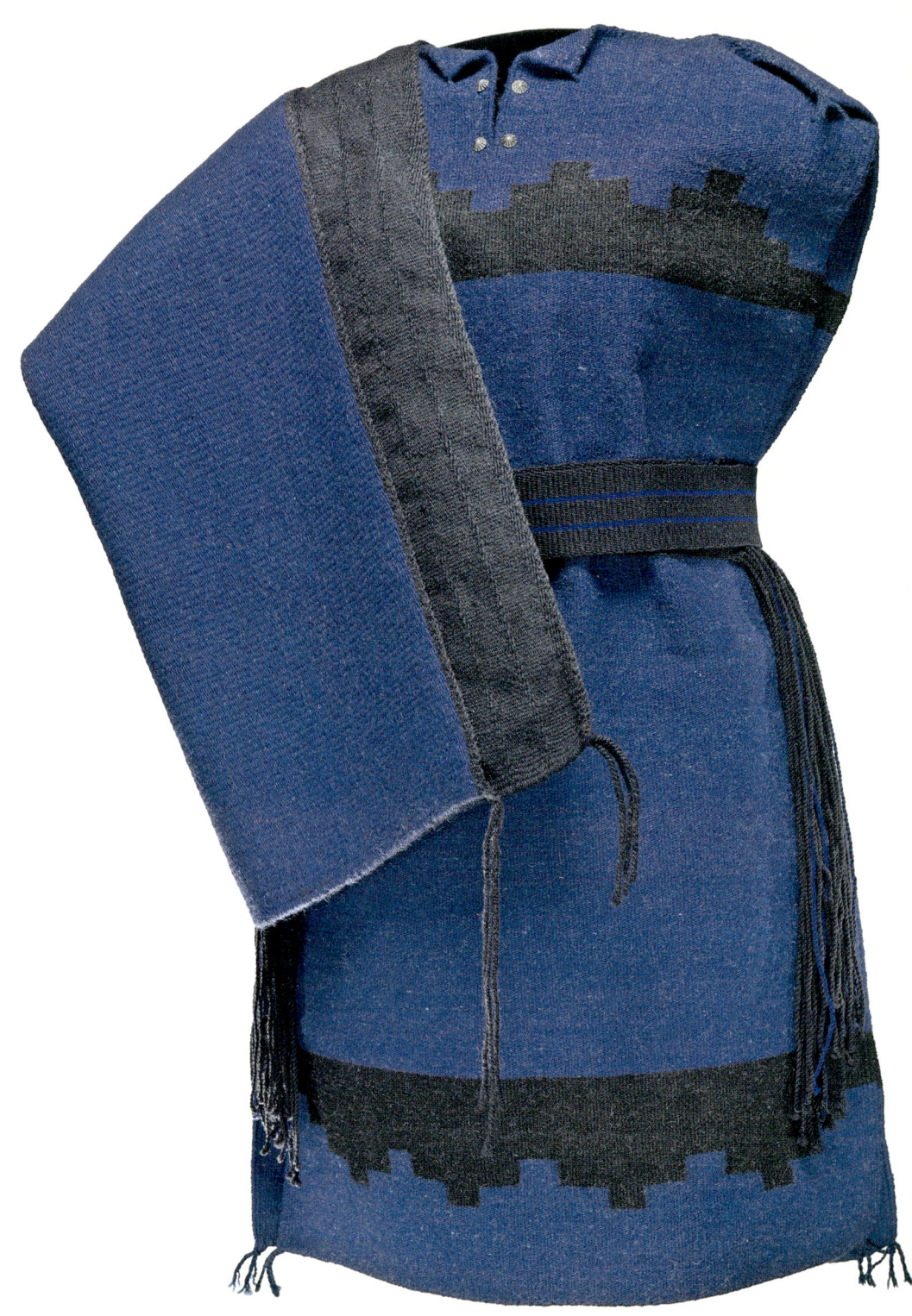

NOVEMBER · DECEMBER

DY Begay (Diné [Navajo], b. 1953)
Biil doó Beeldléí: Asdzání Bi Éé' (woman's garment), 2005
Wool, plant dye
Dress: 22⅜ × 37⅜ in. (56.8 × 94.9 cm)
Manta: 25½ × 43½ in. (64.8 × 110.5 cm)
Sash: 3½ × 87½ in. (8.9 × 222.3 cm)
National Museum of the American Indian

According to tapestry artist DY Begay, Diné believe that possessing and wearing a *biil* (traditional woman's dress) makes a Diné woman easy to recognize for the Holy People and that the woven *biil* guarantees her protection, power, and pride. First worn at a young Diné woman's *kinaaldá*, or coming of age ceremony, it signifies femaleness, and Diné woman consider it special, even sacred, to have a *biil* in their closet. DY Begay wove both the *biil* and the double-faced manta; the matching sash was woven by Sherri Lee Sam (Diné) to complete

NOVEMBER
S	M	T	W	T	F	S
						1
2	3	4	5	6	7	8
9	10	11	12	13	14	15
16	17	18	19	20	21	22
23	24	25	26	27	28	29
30

DECEMBER
S	M	T	W	T	F	S
	1	2	3	4	5	6
7	8	9	10	11	12	13
14	15	16	17	18	19	20
21	22	23	24	25	26	27
28	29	30	31

SUNDAY
30

MONDAY
1

TUESDAY
2

WEDNESDAY
3

THURSDAY
4

FRIDAY
5

SATURDAY
6

DECEMBER

SUNDAY
7

MONDAY
8

TUESDAY
9

WEDNESDAY
10

THURSDAY
11

FRIDAY
12

SATURDAY
13

HUMAN RIGHTS DAY

Makeup storage box used by Anna May Wong, before 1930
Wood, metal, glass
8 × 6 × 6 in.
(20.3 × 15.2 × 15.2 cm)
Gift of Anna May Wong
National Museum of American History

Anna May Wong (1905–1961) was the first Chinese American film star in Hollywood. Despite the stereotyping that limited her opportunities, Wong attracted worldwide recognition for her beauty, style, and acting skills. Wong used this makeup box to fashion her image and captivate audiences.

DECEMBER
S	M	T	W	T	F	S
	1	2	3	4	5	6
7	8	9	10	11	12	13
14	15	16	17	18	19	20
21	22	23	24	25	26	27
28	29	30	31			

JANUARY 2026
S	M	T	W	T	F	S
				1	2	3
4	5	6	7	8	9	10
11	12	13	14	15	16	17
18	19	20	21	22	23	24
25	26	27	28	29	30	31

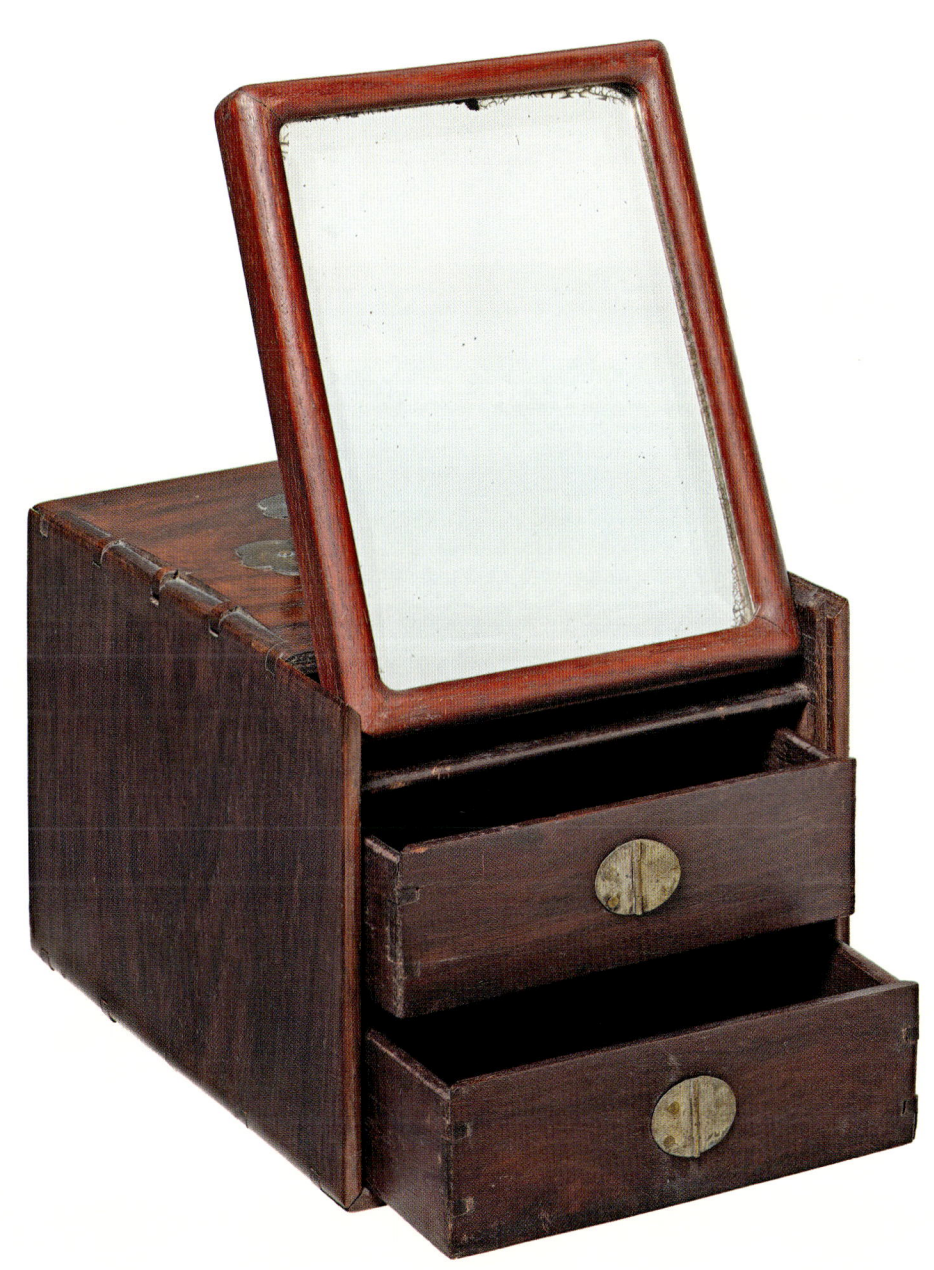

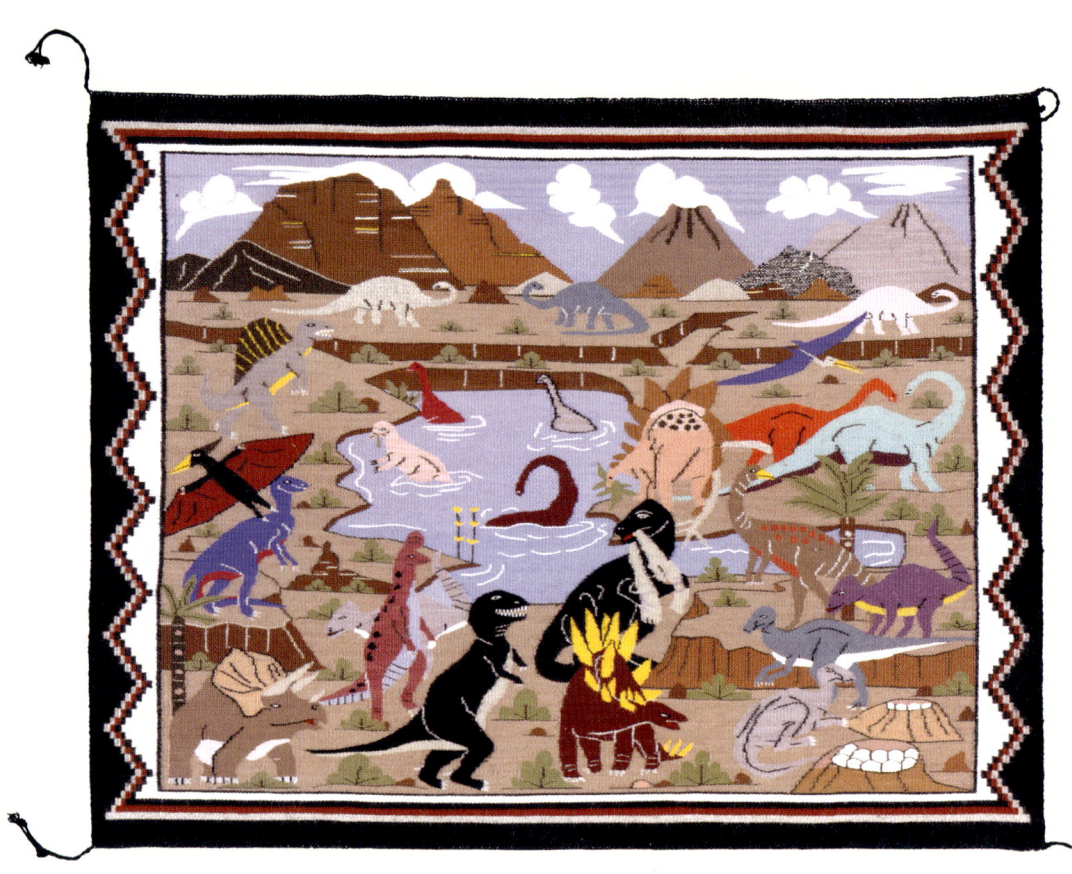

DECEMBER

Florence Riggs
(Diné [Navajo], b. 1962)
Dinosaurs, c. 1993
Commercial yarn
38⅜ × 49⅜ in.
(97.6 × 125.4 cm)
Gift of Chuck
and Jan Rosenak
Smithsonian American
Art Museum

Florence Riggs is the daughter and granddaughter of Navajo weavers and a leader in the contemporary pictorial weaving movement. Her work combines traditional Navajo techniques with modern influences and materials. Her use of commercially dyed yarn gives her work a vibrant palette, and her subject matter is drawn from magazines and popular culture as well as her everyday experiences on the reservation. *Dinosaurs* epitomizes the charming, sometimes cheeky quality of Riggs's body of work.

DECEMBER
S	M	T	W	T	F	S
	1	2	3	4	5	6
7	8	9	10	11	12	13
14	15	16	17	18	19	20
21	22	23	24	25	26	27
28	29	30	31			

JANUARY 2026
S	M	T	W	T	F	S
				1	2	3
4	5	6	7	8	9	10
11	12	13	14	15	16	17
18	19	20	21	22	23	24
25	26	27	28	29	30	31

HANUKKAH BEGINS (SUNDOWN)

SUNDAY 14

MONDAY 15

TUESDAY 16

WEDNESDAY 17

THURSDAY 18

● **FRIDAY 19**

SATURDAY 20

DECEMBER

SUNDAY — FIRST DAY OF WINTER
21

MONDAY — HANUKKAH ENDS (SUNDOWN)
22

TUESDAY
23

WEDNESDAY — CHRISTMAS EVE
24

THURSDAY — CHRISTMAS
25

FRIDAY — KWANZAA BEGINS · BOXING DAY (CAN.)
26

SATURDAY ☽
27

Buck Rogers
Police Patrol Ship, 1934
Louis Marx & Co.,
New York, NY
Tin
12½ × 4 × 5 in.
(31.8 × 10.2 × 12.7 cm)
National Air
and Space Museum

This toy was created as merchandise for the popular space-based adventure series featuring Buck Rogers. It started in 1929 as a comic strip (written by Philip Frances Nowlan and illustrated by Dick Calkins) and was followed by a color Sunday strip in 1930 and a radio program in 1932.

DECEMBER
S	M	T	W	T	F	S
	1	2	3	4	5	6
7	8	9	10	11	12	13
14	15	16	17	18	19	20
21	22	23	24	25	26	27
28	29	30	31			

JANUARY 2026
S	M	T	W	T	F	S
				1	2	3
4	5	6	7	8	9	10
11	12	13	14	15	16	17
18	19	20	21	22	23	24
25	26	27	28	29	30	31

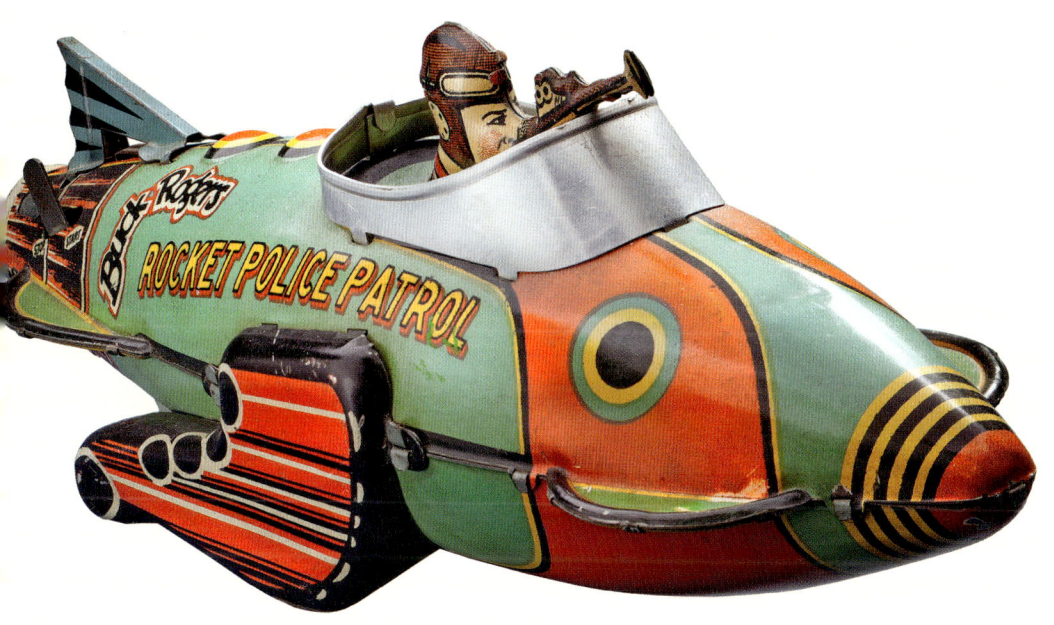

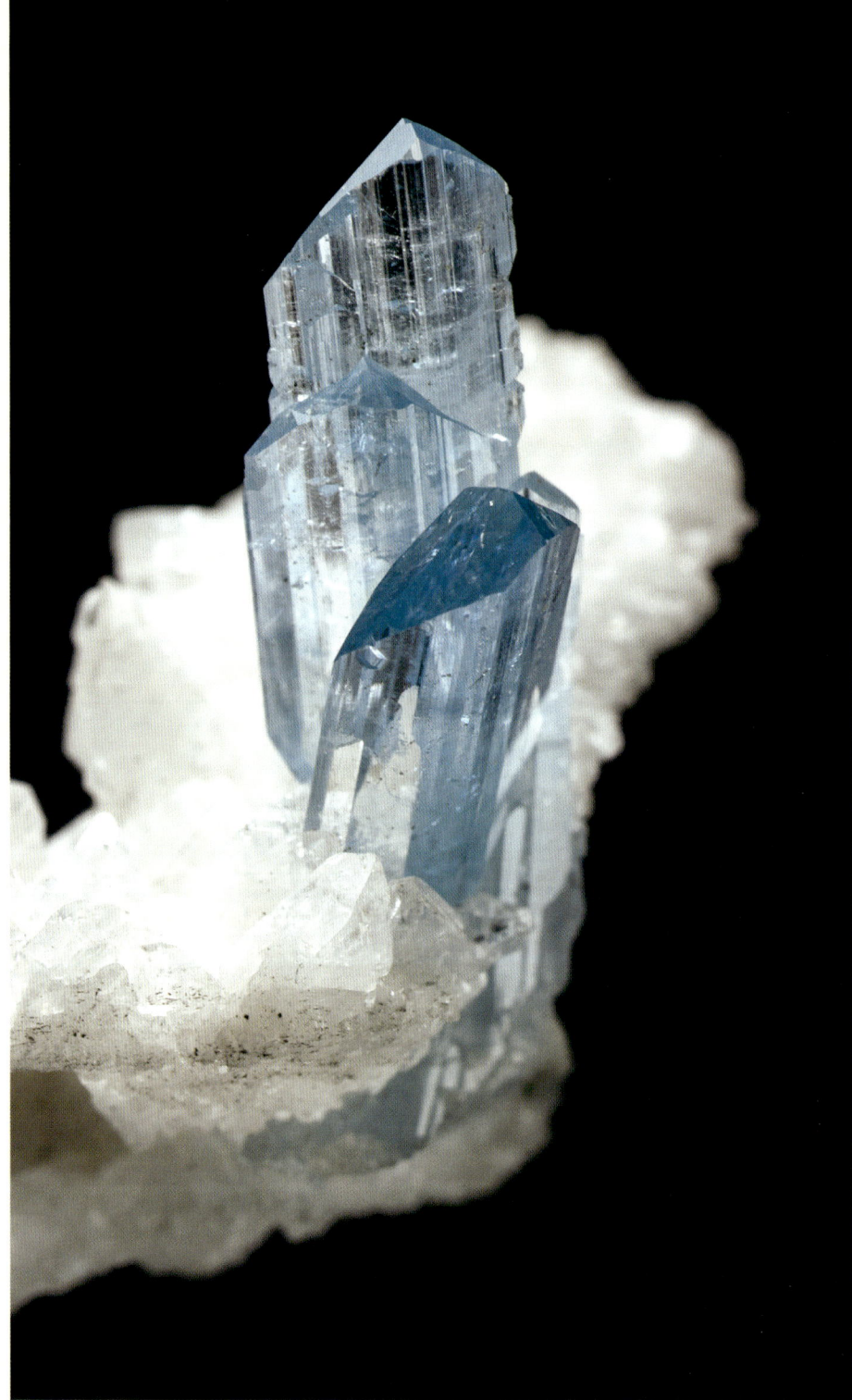

DECEMBER · JANUARY

Euclase with albite
Gachalá, Colombia
2⅝ × 1³⁄₁₆ × 1³⁄₁₆ in.
(6.7 × 3.0 × 2.0 cm)
National Museum
of Natural History

These pale-blue euclase crystals get their name from the Greek words meaning "easily" and "fracture," as the fragile crystals cleave perfectly along precise planes. White albite crystals surround the euclase. This specimen was discovered in Gachalá, Cundinamarca, Colombia, which is famous for producing another impressive crystal in the National Mineral Collection: the 858-carat Gachalá Emerald.

DECEMBER
S	M	T	W	T	F	S
	1	2	3	4	5	6
7	8	9	10	11	12	13
14	15	16	17	18	19	20
21	22	23	24	25	26	27
28	29	30	31			

JANUARY 2026
S	M	T	W	T	F	S
				1	2	3
4	5	6	7	8	9	10
11	12	13	14	15	16	17
18	19	20	21	22	23	24
25	26	27	28	29	30	31

SUNDAY
28

MONDAY
29

TUESDAY
30

NEW YEAR'S EVE

WEDNESDAY
31

NEW YEAR'S DAY · KWANZAA ENDS

THURSDAY
1

FRIDAY
2

SATURDAY
3

SMITHSONIAN NATIONAL MUSEUMS

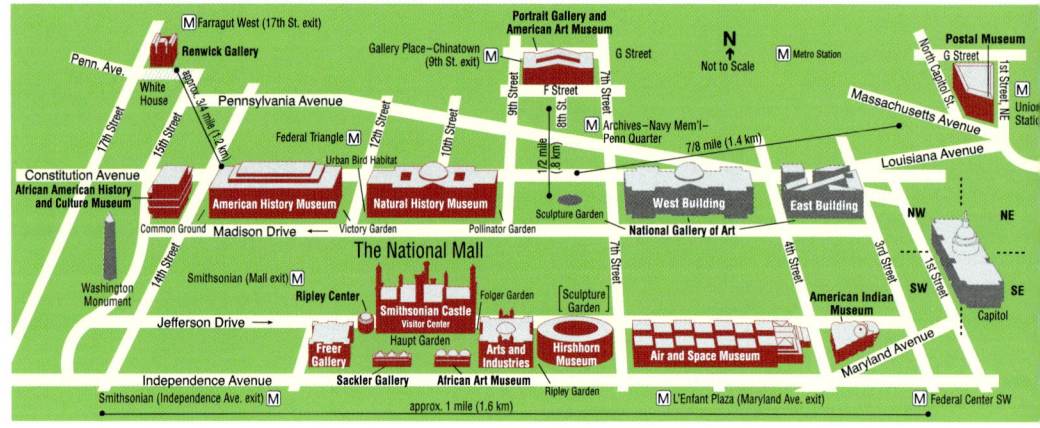

Also in Washington, DC, and Virginia:
Anacostia Community Museum, 1901 Fort Place SE
National Zoological Park, 3001 Connecticut Avenue NW
National Air and Space Museum, Steven F. Udvar-Hazy Center
14390 Air and Space Museum Parkway, Chantilly, Virginia

In New York City:
Cooper Hewitt, Smithsonian Design Museum, 2 East 91st Street and Fifth Avenue
National Museum of the American Indian, George Gustav Heye Center, One Bowling Green

America's Museum—with Global Reach

The Smithsonian Institution is the world's largest museum, education, and research complex. Founded in 1846 through the bequest of Englishman James Smithson (1765–1829), the Smithsonian continues to inspire the present and shape the future by preserving our cultural heritage, discovering new knowledge, and sharing its vast resources with the world.

Visiting the Smithsonian

You may plan your visit via the Smithsonian's website, www.si.edu, or by calling Smithsonian Information at (202) 633-1000 on Monday–Friday, 9 A.M.–5 P.M. For National Zoo information, call (202) 633-4480.

When you arrive in Washington, DC, we encourage you to begin your visit at the Smithsonian's Information Center in the Castle, where you can find maps and brochures in several languages and speak with informed volunteer specialists.

Smithsonian museums in Washington, DC, are open daily, except on December 25. Admission to the Smithsonian museums, the National Zoological Park in Washington, DC, and the National Museum of the American Indian in New York City is free. The admission fee at the Cooper Hewitt, Smithsonian Design Museum is waived for Friends of the Smithsonian. A parking fee is required at the Steven F. Udvar-Hazy Center and at the National Zoo. Refer to the map above for the locations of Smithsonian museums on and near the National Mall in Washington, DC.

For more information on visiting specific museums or centers—and descriptions of programs and exhibitions—please visit the websites listed on the following pages.

We look forward to hosting you.

*Smithsonian Museums and Galleries
on the National Mall, Washington, DC*

Arts and Industries Building
900 Jefferson Drive SW (next to the Castle)
aib.si.edu

The Arts and Industries Building, completed in 1881, housed our country's first national museum. After an extensive renovation, it reopened in 2015 for special events. The Mary Livingston Ripley Garden and a vintage, operational carousel are located nearby.

Hirshhorn Museum and Sculpture Garden
Independence Avenue and 7th Street SW
hirshhorn.si.edu

The Hirshhorn Museum and Sculpture Garden is a leading voice for contemporary art and culture and provides a dynamic platform for the artists, art, and ideas of our time. The collection originated with a bequest from Joseph H. Hirshhorn (1899–1981) and now numbers more than 12,000 artworks. As one of the most-visited modern art museums in the nation, the Hirshhorn activates its mission, "Come as you are, leave transformed" in-person and digitally with a robust series of performances and programs.

National Air and Space Museum
Jefferson Drive between 4th and 7th Streets SW
airandspace.si.edu

The National Air and Space Museum, one of the world's most visited museums, maintains the largest collection of historic aviation and space artifacts, including the original 1903 Wright Flyer, Charles Lindbergh's *Spirit of St. Louis*, and an Apollo lunar module. The Lockheed Martin IMAX Theater's films reveal the wonders of air and space flight.

**National Museum of African
American History and Culture**
1400 Constitution Avenue NW
nmaahc.si.edu

The National Museum of African American History and Culture is a place where all Americans can learn about the richness and diversity of the African American experience. Through historical artifacts, documents, and works of art, the museum's exhibitions tell an American story that unites us all.

National Museum of African Art
950 Independence Avenue SW
africa.si.edu

The National Museum of African Art celebrates Africa's rich culture across time and geography without regional, media, or historical favor. Through its more than 12,000 works of art, as well as the Eliot Elisofon Photographic Archives and the Warren M. Robbins Library, the museum seeks to convey the profound historical and contemporary connections Africa has to the rest of the world.

National Museum of American History
12th Street and Constitution Avenue NW
americanhistory.si.edu

The National Museum of American History seeks to be the most accessible, inclusive, and relevant national history museum. The home of the Star-Spangled Banner, the museum collects and cares for national treasures including the 1830s steam locomotive *John Bull*, First Ladies' gowns, Dorothy's Ruby Slippers, Prince's guitar, Alfred Rascon's Medal of Honor, and other artifacts from America's history.

National Museum of Asian Art
1050 Independence Avenue SW
asia.si.edu

The National Museum of Asian Art opened its doors to the public in 1923 as the United States' first national museum of art. It is home to more than 45,000 objects dating from the Neolithic period to today and originating from the ancient Near East to China, Japan, Korea, South and Southeast Asia, and the Islamic world. The museum also holds a significant group of American works of art largely dating to the late nineteenth century. It also houses the world's largest collection of diverse works by James McNeill Whistler, including the famed Peacock Room, collected by the museum's founder, Charles Lang Freer.

National Museum of Natural History
10th Street and Constitution Avenue NW
naturalhistory.si.edu

The National Museum of Natural History connects people everywhere with Earth's unfolding story. Iconic objects, including the Hope Diamond and the Nation's *T. rex*, and immersive experiences—like Q?rius, the Coralyn W. Whitney Science Education Center, and the live Butterfly Pavilion—attract visitors of all ages, sparking curiosity and illuminating the beauty and wonder of the planet.

National Museum of the American Indian
4th Street and Independence Avenue SW
americanindian.si.edu

The National Museum of the American Indian is dedicated to the preservation and presentation of the diverse arts, history, and material culture of Indigenous peoples of the Western Hemisphere, from the Arctic Circle to Tierra del Fuego. The museum consists of three facilities: the museums on the National Mall and in New York City and the Cultural Resources Center in Suitland, Maryland (open by appointment).

Smithsonian Gardens
gardens.si.edu

The stunning gardens throughout the Smithsonian campus along the National Mall have all been designed to complement the adjacent museums and to enhance visitors' overall learning, appreciation, and enjoyment. The Smithsonian Gardens are open year-round, seven days a week, with the gated Enid A. Haupt Garden behind the Smithsonian Castle open from dawn to dusk.

Smithsonian Institution Building (The Castle)
1000 Jefferson Drive SW
si.edu/museums/smithsonian-institution-building

Popularly known as "the Castle," this building houses the Smithsonian's main offices and the Smithsonian Information Center, where visitors may speak with volunteer information specialists to obtain additional details and directions for museums and the National Zoo.

Smithsonian Museums and Galleries beyond the National Mall in Washington, DC, and Virginia

Anacostia Community Museum
1901 Fort Place SE
anacostia.si.edu

An empowered community controls its destiny. This idea motivates the activities of the Smithsonian's Anacostia Community Museum and drives its mission to illuminate and amplify the community's collective power. The museum serves as a catalyst for critical thought about current issues, convening community stakeholders around shared challenges, common ideals, and collective action.

Lawrence A. Fleischman Gallery of the Archives of American Art
8th and F Streets NW
aaa.si.edu

The Lawrence A. Fleischman Gallery exhibits highlights from the Archives' collection of more than 20 million primary source records, which document two centuries of our nation's artists and art communities.

National Air and Space Museum Steven F. Udvar-Hazy Center
14390 Air and Space Museum Parkway, Chantilly, VA
airandspace.si.edu/udvar-hazy-center

Near Washington Dulles International Airport, the Steven F. Udvar-Hazy Center displays more than 3,000 artifacts, including nearly 200 aircraft. Highlights include a Lockheed SR-71 Blackbird, the Boeing B-29 Superfortress *Enola Gay*, and the Space Shuttle *Discovery*.

National Portrait Gallery
8th and F Streets NW
npg.si.edu

The National Portrait Gallery's more than 26,000 paintings, prints, photographs, drawings, sculptures, and works in new media honor the individuals who have contributed to the history and culture of the United States—and the artists who have portrayed them.

National Postal Museum
2 Massachusetts Avenue NE, next to Union Station
postalmuseum.si.edu

Visitors can experience sorting and delivering the mail and design their own postage stamp at the National Postal Museum, where nearly 6 million objects and dozens of interactive activities present philatelic history, celebrate letter writing, and document the mail-delivery process.

National Zoological Park
3001 Connecticut Avenue NW
nationalzoo.si.edu

The Smithsonian's National Zoo and Conservation Biology Institute inspires commitment to conservation through engaging experiences with animals and the people working to save them. Founded in 1889, the zoo is home to more than 2,700 animals across 390 species, including Asian elephants, Cuban crocodiles, and Panamanian golden frogs.

Renwick Gallery
Smithsonian American Art Museum
Pennsylvania Avenue and 17th Street NW
americanart.si.edu/visit/renwick

The Renwick Gallery is home to the Smithsonian American Art Museum's collection of contemporary craft and decorative art—one of the finest and most extensive collections of its kind. The museum's home is a National Historic Landmark, the first building built expressly as an art museum in the United States.

Smithsonian American Art Museum
8th and F Streets NW
americanart.si.edu

The Smithsonian American Art Museum, the nation's first collection of American art, is home to one of the largest and most inclusive collections of American art in the world. Spanning four centuries, its collections reveal keys aspects of America's rich artistic and cultural history and capture the aspirations, character, and imagination of the American people.

Smithsonian Museums and Galleries in New York City

Cooper Hewitt, Smithsonian Design Museum
2 East 91st Street and Fifth Avenue
cooperhewitt.org

The Cooper Hewitt, Smithsonian Design Museum is steward of one of the world's most diverse and comprehensive design collections—over 215,000 objects spanning thirty centuries. Housed in the landmark Carnegie Mansion, the Cooper Hewitt welcomes everyone to discover the importance of design and its power to change the world.

National Museum of the American Indian
One Bowling Green
americanindian.si.edu/visit/newyork

Nearly 1 million objects collected by George Gustav Heye (1874–1957) form the heart of the collection and represent the cultures of Indigenous peoples of the Western Hemisphere. Housed in the Alexander Hamilton US Custom House, the center offers exhibitions, public programs, performances, and symposia.

Under Development

In 2020, Congress authorized the establishment of two new museums in Washington, DC. Planning is underway for both museums, and it may take more than a decade before they open to the public. Information about pre-opening exhibits, public programs, and additional online content can be found at the websites listed below.

National Museum of the American Latino
latino.si.edu/museum

The National Museum of the American Latino will display the rich history of Latino communities in America and showcase Latino contributions to American history, art, culture, and science.

Smithsonian American Women's History Museum
womenshistory.si.edu

The Smithsonian American Women's History Museum will amplify the stories of American women to acknowledge and empower a diversity of women's voices and recognize women's accomplishments, the history they made, and the communities they represent.

Smithsonian Research and Education

Listed below are Smithsonian units and programs that pursue research and expand knowledge in the sciences, interpret and celebrate American and worldwide culture and traditions, and develop innovative educational programs and ways to deliver information to audiences near and far. Some of these programs present temporary exhibitions open to the public in Washington and across our national Affiliate Museums.

Smithsonian Research Centers

Archives of American Art
Washington, DC
aaa.si.edu

The Archives is the world's largest resource for the study of American art, with more than 6,000 manuscript collections and 2,500 oral histories ranging from the 18th century to the present, and more than 250 collections available online.

Center for Astrophysics | Harvard & Smithsonian
Cambridge, MA
cfa.harvard.edu/sao

The Center for Astrophysics | Harvard & Smithsonian (CfA), which includes the Smithsonian Astrophysical Observatory, is one of the largest astrophysics institutions in the world. The CfA develops and operates ground-based telescopes and space telescopes including the NASA Chandra X-ray Observatory, the NASA TEMPO satellite, and the SWEAP instrument on the Parker Solar Probe.

Center for Folklife and Cultural Heritage
Washington, DC
folklife.si.edu

The center's annual Smithsonian Folklife Festival, Smithsonian Folkways Recordings, Culture Vitality Program, Ralph Rinzler Folklife Archives, exhibitions, films, and symposia promote cultural engagement and understanding.

Museum Conservation Institute
Suitland, MD
si.edu/mci

State-of-the-art analytical techniques are used to study the provenance, composition, and cultural context of artistic, anthropological, and historical objects.

Smithsonian Conservation Biology Institute
Front Royal, VA
nationalzoo.si.edu/conservation

In partnership with the National Zoo, the institute's scientists are leaders in the study, protection, and restoration of threatened species, habitats, and ecosystems.

Smithsonian Environmental Research Center
Edgewater, MD
serc.si.edu

This is the world's leading research center for environmental studies of the coastal zone, and its research spans global change and the effects of chemicals on our landscape.

Smithsonian Libraries and Archives
Washington, DC
librariesarchives.si.edu

The Smithsonian Libraries and Archives is a system of 21 library branches and an institutional archives. It maintains a collection of almost 3 million library volumes and 44,000 cubic feet of archival materials. The Libraries and Archives serves as an educational resource for the Smithsonian Institution, the global research community, and the public.

Smithsonian Marine Station
Fort Pierce, FL
sms.si.edu

The station specializes in studies of Florida's marine biodiversity and ecosystems.

Smithsonian Tropical Research Institute
Republic of Panama
stri.si.edu

The institute studies tropical biodiversity and its importance to human welfare, trains students to conduct research in the area, and promotes conservation by increasing public awareness of tropical ecosystems.

Smithsonian Education and Access

Office of Fellowships and Internships
si.edu/ofi

Smithsonian staff guide the independent research of graduate students and doctoral candidates.

Smithsonian Affiliations
affiliations.si.edu

This national outreach program establishes long-term museum partnerships to share collections and resources.

Smithsonian American Women's History Initiative
womenshistory.si.edu

A pan-institutional effort with a digital-first mission, this initiative seeks to amplify women's voices, honor their past and current achievements, and empower future leaders.

Smithsonian Asian Pacific American Center
smithsonianapa.org

The Center is committed to documenting, celebrating, and sharing the rich and diverse art, history, and culture of Asian American, Native Hawaiian, and Pacific Islander peoples and communities.

Smithsonian Associates
smithsonianassociates.org

The nation's largest museum-based education program annually presents 750 tours, performances, and seminars.

Smithsonian Center for Learning and Digital Access
learninglab.si.edu/about

The center creates models and methods to empower learners to bring ideas to life through Smithsonian resources.

Smithsonian Institution Traveling Exhibition Service
sites.si.edu

This service creates exhibitions that bring knowledge, discovery, and experiences to people across America and beyond.

Smithsonian Latino Center
latino.si.edu

In collaboration with Smithsonian museums, the center celebrates Latino art, history, culture, and scientific achievements and manages Latino leadership programs.

Smithsonian Science Education Center
ssec.si.edu

The center transforms the teaching and learning of K–12 science in American classrooms and beyond.

Smithsonian Enterprises

Smithsonian Enterprises generates income in support of the Smithsonian's mission. Learn more about Smithsonian Enterprises at smithsonian.com.

Smithsonian Retail includes the museum retail stores, IMAX theaters, licensed commercial products, Smithsonian Books trade publishing, the e-commerce website smithsonianstore.com and the Smithsonian direct mail-order catalog, restaurants, and other visitor concessions.

Smithsonian Media include *Smithsonian* magazine and online web services and the Smithsonian TV Channel and Digital Studio.

Smithsonian Travel is made up of Smithsonian Journeys adult educational travel and Smithsonian Student Travel.

Notes

Notes

Notes

Notes

Notes

Notes

Notes

Notes

Notes